The Mystical Poetry

of

Thomas Traherne

The Mystical Poetry

of

Thomas Traherne

by A. L. Clements

Harvard University Press
Cambridge, Massachusetts
1969

For Irma

Let Live

Preface

After only six decades since Thomas Traherne's poetry and prose *Centuries* were first published, it is now common to value his justly esteemed prose above his relatively neglected poetry. In an otherwise perceptive essay on the *Centuries,* Elizabeth Jennings expresses the standard critical view: "Traherne's formal, disciplined poems lack the accessibility, the immediacy of his *Centuries of Meditations.* It is as if the poetic forms were a barrier to the content and we, his readers, can seldom penetrate that barrier." I am not concerned with a comparison of his prose and poetry but do want each to be rightly valued. So far, the poetry has not been. And since in the past there has been no thoroughgoing study of Traherne's poetry, critics seem all too ready to disavail themselves of the pleasures and insights of his poetry. Perhaps we have not as yet that key which would make of the "forms" not a barrier but a gateway to the content. Perhaps Traherne's poetry is undervalued largely because, in addition to not realizing fully the extent of his brother Philip's editorial meddling, we have not yet clearly understood the specific mode of Thomas' poetic expression, the precise nature and meaning of the poems' mystical content, and, especially, the organic relation of content to form and style. Similarly, it usually has not been sufficiently recognized that Thomas' autograph poems, the Dobell Folio poems, are a unified sequence, not a collection of miscellaneous verses; they make their deepest impact when read in a particular way as parts of a continuous whole. Moreover, Traherne's most important works — *Centuries,* the *Poems,* and *Christian Ethicks* — form a body of writings which are amazingly sustained and interrelated variations on his major theme, the central theme of his mystical tradition. If we are truly to appreciate any one flower, we must be conscious of the tree and the ground it grows in. The full measure, therefore, of Traherne's stature as a poet requires an extended study of the mode and meaning of the Dobell Folio poems and their unity and interrelationships, all fully and properly understood in the elucidating context of Traherne's most relevant other work and of the ancient and yet contemporary tradition in which he wrote and lived.

Although Thomas Traherne may impress us as a highly autobiographical and unquestionably sincere poet (who was not writing merely for the exercise nor for fame), we must, for professional reasons, distinguish between poet and speaker and must also respect the aesthetic integrity of the poems. These are necessary and extremely important initial critical, scholarly acts. Thus, for strict critical and scholarly purposes, this study claims not that Traherne was a mystic but that (fine distinction!) the speaker in at least one of his voices was a mystic or, better and more precisely, that the poetry is mystical and best understood as such. Hence the title of this book: "The Mystical Poetry of Thomas Traherne," not "The Poetry of Thomas Traherne, Mystic." But it would be arbitrary, if not willfully blind, to deny entirely all relationship between literature and life or to deny that we can sometimes glimpse the man in and behind the poetry. And so, though the biographical facts are scarce indeed, I do not hesitate to declare my personal conviction that Thomas Traherne the man and poet was a mystic gifted with both philosophical and literary genius.

Because, as I believe further, a major end of Traherne's poetry is to give his readers some insight into that mystical experience which he himself enjoyed, a critic who is unsympathetic to or antagonistic toward mysticism may have some difficulty in being entirely objective. We do well to reflect upon Bertram Dobell's remark: "though it is certainly not necessary that any one who writes about Traherne should believe all that he did, it is yet desirable that he should be generally in sympathy with the faith of which our author was so earnest a professor." By "faith" I read "Christian mystical faith," the exact meaning of which will become clear in the course of this study; and I have tried to be both sympathetic and objective, to give Traherne's poetry what it has not previously received: the best reading it deserves.

ACKNOWLEDGMENTS

I should like to express appreciation for the professional help and encouragement of my friends, colleagues, and former teachers. Robert A. Durr, James H. Elson, Sheldon N. Grebstein, Arthur W. Hoffman, Barry D. Targan, and two readers for Harvard University Press read one or another version of the manuscript; Bernard S. Levy and John D. Walker read parts of the manuscript; and all offered useful advice. I am conscious of the valuable contributions which are theirs and of the shortcomings which are my own. My greatest debts are to Robert Durr, and go beyond the early and continuing guidance which he gave to my study of Traherne, and beyond the high standards of scholarly and critical excellence which he, as teacher and scholar, has provided. I believe he knows all that I thank him for.

The Research Foundation of the State University of New York supported the completion of my manuscript with an award of a fellowship and grant-in-aid, for which I am grateful.

I wish also to thank James M. Osborn, who very kindly permitted me to examine the new Traherne manuscript of "Select Meditations" in the Osborn Collection, Yale University Library, and to quote from this important discovery. Permissions were kindly granted by Oxford University Press to quote from H. M. Margoliouth's edition of *Thomas Traherne: Centuries, Poems, and Thanksgivings;* and by Faber and Faber Ltd. to reprint passages from *Meister Eckhart: Selected Treatises and Sermons,* translated by James M. Clark and John V. Skinner.

Finally, in numerous ways my wife has, over a period of years, helped and encouraged me much more than I can easily or briefly say. The dedication begins to express my gratitude and love.

A. L. C.

Binghamton, 1968

Contents

ABBREVIATIONS USED IN TEXT

C   *Centuries*

CE   *Christian Ethicks*

D   Dobell Folio (Bodleian MS. Eng. poet. c. 42). Thomas Traherne's autograph poems.

F   *Poems of Felicity* (British Museum MS. Burney 392). Philip Traherne's version of his brother's poems.

The Mystical Poetry

of

Thomas Traherne

Introduction. Criticism of Traherne

They wholly mistake the nature of Criticism who think its business is principally to find fault. Criticism . . . was meant a standard of judging well; the chiefest part of which is, to observe those excellencies which should delight a reasonable reader.

John Dryden

CRITICISM OF THOMAS TRAHERNE's poetry has too often been marked by error of fact, gross misunderstanding, uncritical repetition, and exceedingly faulty judgment. Partly because Traherne is but a late discovery, he has been the most misunderstood and the least appreciated of the seventeenth-century poets with whom he is usually associated. But only partly. There are several other substantial reasons for the critical confusion surrounding Traherne's poetry.

One of the most important reasons for the confusion is that, in H. M. Margoliouth's words, the "editing and changing of the text" by Philip Traherne, Thomas' brother, "is a disaster,"[1] a disaster not always or fully understood by critics and editors of Traherne. When Bertram Dobell edited and published in 1903 Thomas' autograph poems (Bodleian MS. Eng. Poet. c. 42, hereafter referred to as the Dobell Folio and as D), Philip's versions were of course then unknown and undiscovered.[2] The highly favorable early critical response to Dobell's edition contrasts significantly, therefore, with the later much less favorable and often negative criticism of Traherne's poetry after Philip's versions were edited by H. I. Bell and published in 1910 under the title *Traherne's Poems of Felicity* (British Museum MS. Burney 392, hereafter referred to as F). Because Bell did not see how destructive Philip's tampering was, his influential judgments, which set the tone and tenor of much subsequent criticism, are too often unknowingly but actually of Philip's revisions, not of Thomas' poetry. Essentially, Bell's view is that "it is probably true to say that Traherne is not primarily a poet at all . . . Not infrequently we meet with the flattest of prose; and very rarely is there any vital connexion between form and content."[3] To illustrate "the flattest of prose," Bell quotes from "Churches II":

> Of Ladies too a shining Host
> If not on Hors-back, in a Coach. (ll. 21–22)

3

This is unquestionably the flattest of prose, but it is Philip's not Thomas': as Margoliouth notes (II, 372), Philip "reintroduced the ladies in line 21. He may also be responsible for their 'Coach' in line 22. He certainly refashioned the whole passage." [4]

It would be more accurate, I believe, to say not that the sometimes incautious and subjective enthusiasm of Dobell and the early reviewers and critics before 1910 excessively inflated Traherne's reputation, but that the failure of many later critics to estimate properly the nature and extent of Philip's editing has unjustly deflated Thomas' poetic stature. After 1910, critics indiscriminately quoted and referred to Thomas' and Philip's versions, now one, now the other, and often Philip's when instead Thomas' could and should have been cited. Unaware of the "disaster" perpetrated by Philip, many critics tended simply to re-sound Bell's judgments, especially on form and content, and monotonously to repeat the charge of repetition or monotony.[5] In all of this criticism one finds no detailed explanation of what specifically is meant by the supposed lack of connection between form and content, and no thoroughgoing, precise discussion of the poetry and mysticism.

Gladys Wade's edition of *The Poetical Works,* the standard edition between 1932 and 1958, compounded the confusion, for it was based upon her mistaken belief that "it is obvious that his [Philip's] corrections as a whole are marked improvements."[6] Like other critics, Miss Wade also began her evaluation of Traherne's poetry by quoting at length and with approval Bell's criticisms. But she elided his frequently reiterated notion that "very rarely is there any vital connexion between form and content." Two pages later, she concluded, without any quotation marks, "Thus for Traherne there is not a vital connection between form and content," and then repeated the same charge in the next paragraph.[7] This, in essence, is the sum and substance of negative criticism of Traherne's poetry by a foremost editor-critic of Traherne and many of his critics. Apart from its being unsound in its origin (Bell, unknowingly judging a corrupt text), it is also untrue, as close examination of Thomas Traherne's poetry will demonstrate.

In my view, purist though it may seem, the fact that Philip meddled renders, for strict critical purposes, the poems found only in F of little worth *in themselves* in measuring Traherne's poetic stature or attempting to comprehend his mysticism: where we have only F versions, we cannot know with certainty what poems, stanzas, and lines are entirely Thomas'. Criticism will be able to realize thoroughly the nature and extent of Philip's destructive revisions only after Thomas' D poetry has been fully analyzed and also carefully compared, where possible, with the edited versions; and then, allowing for the damage done by Philip, even the F poems may in the future somehow ultimately further enhance our understanding of Thomas Traherne.

Many critics not only have simply repeated Bell's erroneous judgments but also have ignored or have failed to realize fully the import of Dobell's early and crucial insight: "yet all the poems I have mentioned, fine as they are when standing alone, gain considerably when they are read as parts of a continuous poem, the subject of which is the history of the author's progress in his pilgrimage towards the kingdom of perfect Blessedness." [8] In other words, the Dobell Folio is, as this book shall demonstrate, a unified, coherent sequence of poems. Only recently have critics begun in part the task of more accurately appreciating the formal qualities of Traherne's poetry. In 1956, Jean-Jacques Denonain discussed the careful linking and ordering of the Dobell Folio poems. Two years later, noting Denonain's work and building on the foundation of Louis Martz's valuable *The Poetry of Meditation,* John Malcolm Wallace contended that "the thirty-seven poems of the Dobell Folio MS . . . constitute a complete five-part meditation which fulfills all the major conditions of a Jesuit exercise." Wallace correctly added that the whole sequence is "a sustained effort on a single theme . . . regeneration is the governing motif"; and he suggested that the titles themselves indicate the grouping of the poems into five sections.[9]

While the insights of Denonain and Wallace on the Dobell sequence are in general of the utmost importance, some qualifications, particularly about meditation, must be made. It is notable that apart from incidental reference Martz does not discuss Traherne in *The Poetry of Meditation*. Though the meditative tradition may "lie behind" Traherne's writing and though Traherne may even have used, in a general way, its three- and five-fold structures, Traherne should not be narrowly designated a meditative poet in the Ignatian-Scholastic tradition, for in manner and substance he is best understood, I believe, as a mystical poet in the broader Christian contemplative tradition. In *The Paradise Within*, however, Martz discusses the Augustinian meditative tradition, a tradition deriving from Augustine through St. Bonaventure, as it applies to Traherne's *Centuries*.[10] Though I give different and less emphasis to the significance of memory and conceptualizing reason in Traherne, the larger sense of "meditative" in *The Paradise Within* comes much closer to the meaning of "mystic" or "contemplative" as used in this book.

When a critic attempts to apply "meditation" or "meditative structure" in the strict sense, particularly of composition, analysis, colloquy, and the corresponding three powers of the soul, he is apt to encounter difficulties.[11] Specifically, Wallace's designating the childhood theme of the four opening poems as Traherne's "composition of place" seems too great an interpretative liberty. And in discussing the last group of poems, Wallace contends that Traherne's concept of God results "in a distortion of the meditation." That is, the critic begins with a rigid pattern, and then when the poetry does not conform to it he berates the poet. Might not the distortion lie in trying to fit Traherne's poetry into an uncongenial mold and pattern, one which Traherne did not in fact attempt to follow strictly? Wallace unknowingly admits as much, in a context which is pejorative in connotation and unnecessarily harsh, when he writes that Traherne "is already regenerated before he begins." [12] Precisely! Having himself achieved Felicity, Traherne is more concerned to reveal its meaning to others than to work himself up to a state of devotion. He writes out of, not toward, the mystic experience.

The Dobell Folio may appear meditational because, although Traherne writes from the heightened perspective of the mystic pilgrim who has himself found his way Home, he writes of his own spiritual history and he writes not only to but also for those of his fellow men who have not progressed spiritually as far as he. In a sense, the speaker of the poems is Everyman. And in trying to lead others up to Felicity, Traherne may certainly have availed himself, in a general way, of the meditational ladder of ascent. Like any cultivated, highly educated man of his time, and as some of his early work suggests, Traherne must have had some knowledge of meditative patterns. We should, however, not demand that Traherne follow strictly these patterns but rather expect that he would have reshaped them to meet his own particular philosophic and poetic needs. After all, in such reshaping of traditional forms, a poet's uniqueness and originality reveal themselves.

There is, then, a twofold perspective, a double voice in the Dobell Folio. Such a voice both directs the way and keeps the goal immediately and effectively before us. When writing spiritual autobiography, or when speaking for his fellow man, Traherne's *assumed* voice is often that of a man who has not yet attained to Felicity. Yet there are cogent evidences that Traherne not only traveled the *via mystica* (which alone would distinguish his poetry as mystical) but also reached at least as far as illumination and, very probably, arrived at the contemplative's final destination, union. The view that Traherne wrote both *for* and *to* others out of his own achieved mystic experience can, I think, best help to explain the presence in the Dobell Folio of, for example, sudden shifts of tense, outbursts of ecstatic passages, and that marked pervasive Joy which is the unmistakable sign and fruit of mysticism, of Traherne's being "already regenerated."

An inadequate understanding of Traherne's traditional mysticism (his "content") is yet another reason for the failure to appreciate his poetry and to perceive the organic relation in it between form and content. The great majority of discussions of his mystical philosophy is to be found in general works on mysticism, literary histories, introductions, and notes rather than in extended, detailed studies. The nature of his mysticism has only been briefly sketched or, in the case of several longer studies, inaccurately portrayed, never fully and precisely described. On the whole, discussions of Traherne's mysticism are general, superficial, and disappointing; like the studies of his poetic qualities, many of these discussions tend simply to repeat and elaborate earlier criticisms.[13]

The common serious misapprehensions of Traherne's theme of childhood and the repeated allegations of egocentrism and subjectivism clearly reveal the critical failure to grasp Traherne's mystical philosophy. Some of the earliest critics took the central theme of childhood in a biographical, sentimentally nostalgic, and too literal sense. Thereafter, it was also often mistaken as a kind of solipsism or as psychological regression. But an explanation of the theme of childhood is to be found neither in these views nor in the mid-seventeenth-century disappointment with Renaissance faith in knowledge nor in "Enthusiastic" revolt against culture and learning. There can be no question that the meaning of childhood in Traherne is biblical in origin, mystical in tradition, and

symbolic in import. As early as 1934, J. B. Leishman recognized
its scriptural origin in a passing reference to the necessity of becoming as little children to enter the kingdom of Heaven. And
in 1947, Allan H. Gilbert cited not only Matthew 18:2–3 but also
other pertinent biblical passages and warned against being too
literal-minded in reading Traherne and thereby failing to understand his "metaphor of childhood," for Traherne's "child is essentially a symbol." [14] Nevertheless, much Traherne criticism has remained indifferent to or insufficiently aware of the full biblical,
mystical, and symbolic significance of childhood.

Assertions about Traherne's egocentrism and subjectivism ignore
the profound grasp he must have had throughout his mature years
of the nature of humility and of the centrally and pervasively important *psyche-pneuma* distinction, a distinction the critics nowhere make.[15] Traherne's irrepressible exuberance and felicity
must not be mistaken for pride or egocentrism or subjectivity, because humility and joy are not incompatible. True, until very
recently, we did not have available the newly discovered manuscript of "Select Meditations," apparently written between 1660
and 1665, in which Traherne writes that "Humility is . . . the
Basis of every vertue, it is a certain seasoning of felicity, that give
a Relish, and Diviner Tast to all our Joys." [16] But one could have
read the chapter entitled "Humility is the basis of all Vertue and
Felicity" in *Christian Ethicks,* published in 1675, the year after
Traherne's death. I believe that, as a consequence of his years of
effort toward spiritual self-perfection, what an enlightened, felicitous man like Traherne responds to and sees in other men, the
world, and himself is *pneuma;* and that Traherne's Christian
philosophy is founded finally not on love of self (meaning *psyche*)
but on love of the real Self, which is in the image of God, on
love of *pneuma,* which divine reality underlies and pervades the
entire universe.

Whereas earlier critics like T. O. Beachcroft and Wade recognized that Traherne's tradition was Christian-mystical-Neoplatonic, some later critics have separated him too sharply from that tradition or have regarded him as a mystic only in a highly qualified or nontraditional sense.[17] By placing Traherne in the line of medieval mystical tradition, particularly that of St. Bernard and Cistercian mysticism, K. W. Salter helps, in his recent book, to re-establish a part of the larger context in which Traherne should properly and can most fruitfully be regarded. Examining the *Centuries* from this perspective and focusing on Traherne's doctrine of love, Salter cogently makes in his chapter entitled "The Great Hierophant" several positive contributions to the study of Traherne's thought. He demonstrates that Traherne's "sense of union with God" is expressed in terms of love; that love for Traherne is the creative and perfective power by which the real Self or God is attained; that "love, enjoyment and knowledge form a trinity of meaning in Traherne's mystical experience"; and that Traherne's view of self-love as leading to the love of God very closely resembles the doctrines of Christian love found in St. Bernard and his disciples. From this discussion Salter is then able to refute those critics who mistakenly regard Traherne as facilely optimistic, to show that Traherne does not sentimentally minimize the fact of evil, and to argue persuasively that taken in their context Traherne's words express not Panglossian complacency but the mystic awareness which sees good and evil as part of a larger divine pattern. Against Salter's conclusions on the limitations of Traherne's mysticism, however, this present study will attempt to show that Traherne also knew the stages of purgation and, very likely, union and that he was a contemplative, not merely "a visionary" nor merely "an exponent of meditation."[18]

Apart from occasional references to or quotations of the poetry, eight of the nine chapters in Salter's book mainly treat the *Cen-*

turies and only one short chapter considers the poetry. Although Salter cites Margoliouth's text when quoting the poetry, he indiscriminately refers to F poems, quotes F versions instead of D when both are available, and, as Quiller-Couch did in his anthology of Traherne, even mixes lines from D and F in the same poem. To illustrate "Traherne at his most characteristic, and at his best," he quotes "Hosanna," a poem which exists only in Philip's version. Thus he is guilty of the same textual confusion as Bell and many subsequent critics. It is no wonder then that Salter's main thesis and conclusion concerning the poetry is that it "is less fine than the experience," which is but another version of the all-too-familiar form-content bifurcation.[19]

Not only has disastrous editing distorted Traherne's poetry since the time of his death, but much faulty scholarship and unoriginal, unimaginative criticism have misrepresented, misunderstood, and needlessly deprecated it and his mystical philosophy, almost invariably failing "to observe those excellencies which should delight a reasonable reader." Clearly, then, there is need for reconsideration and more thorough discussion of such matters as the crucial differences between Thomas' and Philip's versions, the order, qualities, and excellencies of the autograph poems, the relation in these poems of form and content, Traherne's major theme of childhood or regeneration, his supposed egocentrism and subjectivism, his central ideas (for example, the *psyche-pneuma* distinction) and the nature of his mysticism — all of which will be treated in the following chapters.

One. Traherne's Vision and Tradition: Context of Meaning

*Our Saviors Meaning, when He said, He must be Born
again and becom a little Child that will enter into the
Kingdom of Heaven: is Deeper far then is generaly
believed.*

Centuries

All the stirrings of Grace and Nature, all the acts of GOD
*and the Soul, all his Condescensions, and beginnings to
advance us, all his Gifts at their first coming, all the depths
and changes of our Condition, all our Desires, all our
primitive and virgin Joyes,* the whole story of our Creation, and Life, and Fall, and Redemption, *in all the new-
ness of its first appearance, all our Wants and Dangers,
Exigencies and Extremities, all our Satisfactions and Delights are* present together in our Humility. (*Emphasis
supplied.*)

Christian Ethicks

It is possible to regard Traherne from the perspective of the *Philosophia Perennis,* in that term's sense of worldwide mysticism. Such an approach would discover and discuss the universal patterns into which Traherne's mystical thought and art fall and would doubtlessly prove interesting and fruitful. But to take the stance required by this telescopic perspective might well raise for some readers as many difficulties and problems as it resolves by removing parts of our study a little too far from Traherne's own work and religion.[1] On the other hand, though contemporary movements surely had some effect on him and a study of them sheds some light, to view Traherne *only* through restrictive contemporary lenses, as responding to Puritanism, as being influenced by or sharing affinities with the Cambridge Platonists, the Seekers, the Enthusiasts, the growing Rationalism, or the coming Primitivists, is ultimately to set him out of focus, to regard him in half-light at best and so to see him but dimly.

The context most pertinent and enlightening for the study of Traherne is, I believe, the rich and complex Christian contemplative or mystical tradition, with which his own vision is most in accord. This is to imply that Traherne's most important actual or probable sources and influences, direct or indirect, are the Bible, Plato, Plotinus, Early Church Fathers (particularly Augustine and Dionysius the pseudo-Areopagite), and Renaissance Humanists (particularly Pico della Mirandola and Marsilio Ficino); and that to these one should add, not necessarily as direct sources and influences but at least as spiritual brethren of Traherne's, such names as Richard of St. Victor, St. Bonaventura, Meister Eckhart, Henry Suso, John Ruysbroeck, the author of *The Cloud of Unknowing,* Julian of Norwich, and Jacob Boehme, to list in chronological order but a few Christian mystics among the many contemplatives whose major ideas correspond closely to Traherne's and whose writings may therefore illuminate his works.

There is a vital matter of correct proportion and emphasis to be observed while considering a writer within a complex, variously interrelated tradition. We shall avoid error and the obscuring of important distinctions by recognizing that Traherne was first and foremost a Christian mystic, secondly a Neoplatonist, and thirdly a Christian Neoplatonic mystic who — like any highly educated, intelligent Christian of his day — was knowledgeable about and incorporated into his work where appropriate elements of Aristotelian and Scholastic thinking. From Book VII of Augustine's *Confessions,* for example, Traherne would have learned something of both the value and the limitations of Platonism. In our efforts to elucidate Traherne's work by means of his tradition, we shall thus make much more frequent reference to Christian contemplatives and Neoplatonists, like Augustine and Eckhart, than to non-Christian ones. Furthermore, like many of the Christian contemplatives of his tradition who were familiar with classical philosophy and who perceived a holy and divine element in the external physical world, Traherne appears to hold an Aristotelian rather than a Platonic view of form and matter and the relation between the two. It is most important to realize that in significant ways Traherne is un-Platonic in his conception of the physical universe, so that whenever we discuss this issue the Hebraic-Christian and Aristotelian elements of Traherne's thought must be given proper and greater emphasis.

A major assumption of this book, then, is that Thomas Traherne's poetry may best be understood and appreciated through the perspective and within the context of Christian mystical tradition, including of course the effect of the Bible, Plato, Neoplatonism, and (to a lesser extent) Aristotelianism on that tradition and Traherne. The great speculative Christian school of mysticism, especially between Eckhart and Boehme, forms a curiously well-integrated tradition (and one which might be considered roughly equivalent to a Christian branch of the Perennial Philosophy). Renaissance and later medieval mystics were familiar with earlier Christian mystics as well as with the Church Fathers and classical writers. Even Plotinus himself, the pagan Neoplatonist who so remarkably affected Christianity, often employs Aristotelian vocabulary, argumentation, and ideas. The numerous strands of Traherne's tradition are more variously and closely interwoven than might at first glance appear.[2]

Since they are fundamental also to Traherne, a few basic "ideas" of his tradition require consideration in this chapter. A discussion of them will provide some general description if not definition of Traherne's kind of mysticism; and an initial grasp of them is essential for a subsequent deeper and fuller appreciation of his poetry. The discussion of these key ideas also will help to clear away certain confusions about his thought and will afford a context of meaning and some terminology for our consideration of his poetic in Chapter 2 and our detailed analysis of his poetry in Chapters 3 to 5. These interrelated ideas concern the theme of childhood; the distinction between *psyche* and *pneuma;* the "meaning" of the Godhead; the negative and positive ways; and what we may call the doctrine of the Golden Mean. In its fullest sense, in its symbolic and mythic dimensions, the theme of childhood can be seen to subsume the other four ideas in that a comprehension of the other four is necessary for a proper or complete understanding of this central theme. Because "childhood," in different senses, is both the main theme and vehicle of the Dobell Folio poems, we shall naturally discuss or refer to it frequently.

One need only read "Blisse," "The Approach," "Shadows in the Water," and *Centuries* IV 6 in order to realize, as is actually everywhere apparent, that Traherne well understood the literal differences between childhood and adulthood, although we should take him at his word that the early childhood and redeemed

experiences, while not identical, are both in some sense "divine." [3]
He knew, as we all do, that children can be grossly egotistical
and are without the patience, kindness, wisdom of adults — some
adults. This point should need no further proving or belaboring.
Childhood is Traherne's major vehicle, an *allegoria* for the regenerated state, and it is an apt one both because actual early childhood may serve the fallen adult as a partial model of redeemed
experience and because the states of childhood and redemption
have in common many analogous conditions and characteristics.
Thus to complain about Traherne's "limited range of subject" or
merely to call him a poet of childhood and leave it at that would
take us little further than saying Donne's "Valediction: Forbidding
Mourning" is a poem about a compass or *King Lear* is a play
about the infirmities of old age. Traherne's deliberate choice of
subject, regeneration, developed greatly through the major metaphor of childhood, is surely wise, for the subject is, at least potentially, of considerable import for every man.

As later chapters attempt to demonstrate, the poems of the
Dobell Folio present a vision of life as threefold: for Traherne,
the spiritual progress of a man's life is, or ideally should be, from
childhood wonder and innocence through fallen adult experience
to blessed Felicity. This movement through qualitatively different
states of Being may be and usually is figured as cyclical or cir-
cular — the circle being the familiar finite symbol of eternity —
and it is to be taken precisely as figurative, symbolic, mythic. There
is a coming back again, as it were, to the beginning, a coming back
again but with a difference. Traditionally, the Bible has been regarded by Christian theologians and mystics as a definitive myth
or mythos extending from Creation to Apocalypse. Its unity depends upon the series of movements related to the process of
creation, fall, redemption (and apocalypse) in the coming (and
second coming) of Christ. In biblical terms, this spiritual pro-

gression, successfully completed, may be spoken of as the regaining of Eden or Paradise, or the recovery of that divine, creative, and redemptive image which is hidden within man. The movement, then, of the Dobell Folio poems from innocence through fallen experience to Felicity is perfectly in accord with and indeed grows out of Christian biblical, mystical tradition: Adam's, Everyman's, progress is from prelapsarian Eden through the Fall to Redemption in Christ.[4] This progress is what we mean — or should mean — by the theme of childhood in Traherne, which, rightly understood, is Traherne's particular individuation of his tradition's overriding archetype of Regeneration.

"Regeneration," as intended here, is the heart of the mystical experience and not just a Christian commonplace. There are, as it were, two "baptisms," one of the letter and the other of the spirit, one of piety and the other mystical, though both are called "regeneration." Baptism of the spirit, regeneration in our sense, is not a merely verbal or intellectual grasp of certain principles nor a merely superficial conversion, but rather that deeply realized, radical, and thoroughgoing change in one's mode of consciousness which is both the beginning and center of the mystic life. This is the kind of regeneration that authoritative writers on mysticism, such as Evelyn Underhill, describe: "The true and definitely mystical life does and must open with that most actual, though indescribable phenomenon, the coming forth into consciousness of man's deeper, spiritual self, which . . . mystical writers of all ages have agreed to call Regeneration or Re-birth." Underhill points out that mystics frequently refer to this phenomenon as "the eternal Birth or Generation of the Son or Divine Word."[5] Quite evidently, for Traherne Rebirth or Regeneration and the theme of becoming as a little child are one and the same, equivalent to the full actualization of our potentialities as Sons of God:

Wisely doth S. John say, We are the Sons of God; but the World knoweth us not becaus it knew Him not. He that Knoweth not the Spirit of God, can never Know a Son of GOD, nor what it is to be His Child. He made us the sons of GOD in Capacity by giving us a Power, to see Eternity, to Survey His Treasures, to love his children, to know and to lov as He doth, to becom Righteous and Holy as He is; that we might be Blessed and Glorious as He is. The Holy Ghost maketh us the Sons of God in Act, when we are Righteous as He is Righteous, and Holy as He is Holy. When we prize all the Things in Heaven and Earth, as He Prizeth Him, and make a Conscience of doing it as He doth after His similitude; then are we actually present with them, and Blessed in them, being Righteous and Holy, as He is. then the Spirit of GOD dwelleth in us, and then are we indeed the Sons of God, a Chosen Generation, a Royal Priesthood, an Holy Nation, a Peculiar People, Zealous of Good Works, shewing forth the Praises of Him, who hath called us out of Darkness, into His Marvellous Light. (*C* I 99; see also I 60 and IV 70)

Childhood, as Christ certainly understood, is a perfect metaphor for the redeemed state: "Except ye be converted, and become as little children, ye shall not enter into the kingdom of heaven" (Matt. 18:3). Or, in the words of the fourth Evangelist: "Except a corn of wheat fall into the ground and die, it abideth alone: but if it die, it bringeth forth much fruit. He that loveth his life shall lose it; and he that hateth his life in this world shall keep it unto life eternal" (John 12:24–25).[6] Both passages are metaphors for the same transformation, the same experience of hating, giving up, the illusional, egoistic life to realize the life of the true Self or Spirit. This central paradox of gain through loss, of life through death, embodies a traditional distinction important to understanding so much in Traherne: the distinction between the outward and inward man, Greek *psyche* and *pneuma,* Hebrew *nefesh* and *ruach,* the first Adam who is a living soul and the last Adam who is a quickening spirit, the man "himself" and the divine, supra-individual Being.[7] Becoming like unto a child, traveling the *via mystica,* is the highest act of Self-knowledge: it is to undergo the transformation from egohood to Selfhood, to make that spiritual journey whereby man's Divine Image is restored, to be transhumanized, in Dante's phrase, from man into a god.

Beside biblical authority, Traherne had the confirming word of mystical tradition. One of mysticism's fundamental articles of faith is the doctrine, derivative in Christianity from Genesis, that man is made in God's image, that "since we can only know what is akin to ourselves, *man, in order to know God, must be a partaker of the Divine nature.*"[8] The idea that the true Self in the depth of the particular individual is identical with or at least like unto the Divinity is expressed most succinctly in the Sanskrit formula *tat tvam asi* (that art thou) and is found pervasively in mystical literature, though we shall confine ourselves to Traherne's Christian Neoplatonic tradition. In the *Theaetetus,* Plato makes the point that it is only by becoming godlike that we can know God. Plotinus teaches that the soul in its lapse from its original goodness falls into the *regio dissimilitudinis* and must return to God through its likeness to him. For Augustine, who develops from Plotinus this idea of the region of unlikeness, the soul's likeness to God has been restored in the Incarnate Word. Or in the words of St. Athanasius, "God became man that man might become God."[9] Christ is the way and the example; the Resurrection is in and of the Body as well as the Soul. And under the influence of Augustine, "image theology" makes its way to the medieval Christian

writers, who express the essential spiritual unity of man and God
in such terms as the apex of the soul, the ground, the spark, anima,
and synderesis.

The pertinence of all of this to Traherne should be obvious
enough: the child falls from his "Estate of Innocence," his original
goodness or God-likeness, into "Apostasie" (*C* III 2), and in order
to enter again into the kingdom of Heaven he must recover his
innocence, that is to say rediscover his Sonship or inward Self
through Christ. Traherne concludes *Christian Ethicks* with a discussion of God-likeness, which he relates directly to the biblical
inward man, to pneuma in our sense of the term: "Godliness is a
kind of *GOD-LIKENESS,* a divine habit, or frame of Soul, that
may fitly be accounted *The fulness of the stature of the Inward
Man.* In its least degree, it is an Inclination to be Like GOD, to
Please him, and to Enjoy him . . . Every Like in Nature draweth
to its Like, the Beautiful, and the Wise, and the Good, and the
Aged; but especially the *GOD-Like.* There is more reason why
they should delight in each other. They have more Attractives and
Incentives. *GODLINESS,* or *GOD-LIKENESS* is the cement of
Amity between *GOD* and *MAN.* Eternity and Immensity are the
sphere of his Activity, and are often frequented, and filled with
his Thoughts. Nothing less than the Wisdom of *GOD* will please
the *GOD-LIKE Man:* Nothing less content him, than the Blessedness and Glory of his Great Creatour. He must enjoy GOD, or he
cannot enjoy himself." [10] Presumably, a man cannot enjoy himself
unless he enjoys God precisely because of the essential spiritual
unity of God and man, because, at the least, God-likeness is the
real nature of the inward man.

Writing on "the fundamental dogma of mystical psychology,"
Abbé Bremond further clarifies and expands the meaning of "the
distinction between the two selves: *Animus,* the *surface self;*

Anima, the *deep self; Animus,* rational knowledge; and *Anima,* mystical or poetic knowledge . . . the I, who feeds on notions and words and enchants himself by doing so; the Me, who is united to realities." "My Me is God," St. Catherine of Genoa asserts, "nor do I recognize any other Me except my God Himself." "What is life?" Meister Eckhart asks, and boldly affirms: "God's being is my life, but if it is so, then what is God's must be mine and what is mine God's. God's is-ness is my is-ness [*istigkeit*], and neither more nor less." With direct pertinence, the great Flemish mystic Jan van Ruysbroeck makes the psyche-pneuma distinction in the terms of created and uncreated nature: "all men who are exalted above their created nature into a life of contemplation are one with this Divine clarity, and they are the clarity itself. And they behold and feel and discover themselves, by means of this Divine light: they discover that they are this same single deepness, according to the manner of their uncreated nature . . . And so contemplative men attain to that everlasting image in which they are made." [11]

Quotations such as these from the contemplatives could be multiplied indefinitely. They abound in Traherne — especially if we respond rightly to his symbolism and imagery. For example, describing pneuma or "My Spirit" in the poem of that title, the ecstatic fifth stanza exclaims:

> O Joy! O Wonder, and Delight!
>   O Sacred Mysterie!
> My Soul a Spirit infinit!
>   An Image of the Deitie!
>   A pure Substantiall Light!
> That Being Greatest which doth Nothing seem!
> Why twas my All, I nothing did esteem

But that alone. A Strange Mysterious Sphere!
   A Deep Abyss
    That sees and is
The only Proper Place or Bower of Bliss.
   To its Creator tis so near
    In Lov and Excellence
    In Life and Sence,
In Greatness Worth and Nature; And so Dear;
   In it, without Hyperbole,
   The Son and friend of God we see.[12]

The terminology may differ even considerably in various writers of the contemplative tradition, but the idea remains essentially the same, as when, for example, Blake writes with his characteristic directness: "Man is all Imagination. God is Man and exists in us and we in him" ("Annotations to Berkeley's *Siris*"); and, from "The Laocoon," "The Eternal Body of Man is The Imagination, that is, God himself."

    Lest there be a serious confusion, however, a further clarification of the psyche-pneuma distinction is necessary. The principle expressed in *tat tvam asi,* so vital and basic to Traherne's "mystical idealism," does not mean that "therefore, I am God Almighty!" [13] For the "I," psyche, or ego, in our sense of the term, is one's conception of himself, the known created object, not the knowing, creative Act. It is a prideful sense of separate existence, the notion one forms of himself, the role he assumes and is assigned to play, an abstraction and convention rather than the concrete, living Reality. As an illusion, it prevents, as long as one mistakes an echo for the Word, his realizing fully his true nature; and the attempt to preserve, to reify, this ghost (Blake's "Spectre") alienates one still further from the Holy Ghost. The condition of fallen man, then, is the sin, the error, of misapprehending his psyche as his essential being and of behaving, or rather misbehaving, accordingly. After eating the apple, Milton's Adam, thinking only of his bond with Eve and not of his precedential bond with God, "forgets," in effect, who he really is. The isolated ego, this principle of death, must thus be given up and over, must itself die, in order that a process of infinite expansion occur, in order that at-one-ment with God, life eternal, be realized. Putting it another way, by transcending mere individuality, the role-playing ego, we attain inner unity or, paradoxically, our truest individuality. In short, the necessity of purgation has always been a fundamental mystical doctrine.

It is to this need for purgation that Traherne refers in, for example, "The Instruction" and at the beginning of *The Third Century* when he writes of his corruption and of unlearning "the Dirty Devices of this World" (III, 3). In the passage from which one of this chapter's epigraphs is taken, Traherne explicitly relates the theme of childhood to the Fall, as he explains that

Our Saviors Meaning, when He said, He must be Born again and becom a little Child that will enter into the Kingdom of Heaven: is Deeper far then is generaly believed. It is not only in a Careless Reliance upon Divine Providence, that we are to becom Little Children, or in the feebleness and shortness of our Anger and Simplicity of our Passions: but in the Peace and Purity of all our Soul. Which Purity also is a Deeper Thing then is commonly apprehended. for we must disrobe our selvs of all fals Colors, and unclothe our Souls of evil Habits; all our Thoughts must be Infant-like and Clear: the Powers of our Soul free from the Leven of this World, and disentangled from mens conceits and customs. Grit in the Ey or the yellow Jandice will not let a Man see those Objects truly that are before it. And therfore it is requisit that we should be as very Strangers to the Thoughts Customs and Opinions of men in this World as if we were but little Children. So those Things would appear to us only which do to Children when they are first Born. Ambitions, Trades, Luxuries, inordinat Affections, Casual and Accidental Riches invented since the fall would be gone, and only those Things appear, which did to Adam in Paradice, in the same Light, and in the same Colors. God in his Works, Glory in the Light, Lov in our Parents, Men, our selvs, and the Face of Heaven. Evry Man naturaly seeing those Things, to the Enjoyment of which He is Naturaly Born. (*C* III 5)

For Traherne, then, becoming like unto a child includes, among its other meanings, the purgative process whereby the various prideful effects of the Fall (and of every man's fall) are undone and overcome so that one may regain that naked, pure humility which is the true Man or Ground of one's Being,[14] may undergo that humble self-divesting or ego-crucifying which conduces to the Self's highest exaltation.

There is an additional refinement to be made. A wisdom even greater than the doctrine of purgation obtains among the Christian contemplatives of Traherne's tradition and helps to account for their sometimes according larger significance to the Incarnation than to the Crucifixion, even though the Crucifixion is to them so vitally important. They have the abiding and deep awareness that, in Eckhart's words, "nothing is as near to me as God is. God is nearer to me than I am to myself. My being depends on God's intimate presence."[15] Traherne's own words are almost identical: "God is there [in the Soul], and more near to us then we are to our selvs" (*C* II 81). Traherne would have read in the Psalms that "Thou art near, O Lord" (119:151) and would have learned from St. Paul's preaching to the Athenians that God is "not far

from every one of us: for in him we live, and move, and have
our being; as certain also of your own poets have said, For we
are also his offspring" (Acts 17:27–28). "But Thou wert more
inward to me, than my most inward part," St. Augustine similarly affirms, "and higher than my highest." [16] Recognizing the
unworthiness of one's fallen nature, and all that implies, is itself
prelude and key to discovering one's "more near" or "more inward" Being and ultimately to entering wholly into the state of
effulgent beatitude. But only the true Self, not the fallen ego, can
accept and affirm, can act. It even chooses to act as if It were
fallen and in need of crucifixion. God acts and is; man, on his
own, can neither act meaningfully nor be. The psyche is indeed
an illusion, a fiction, however tenaciously it may foolishly persist
in refusing to die and let eternal life be. In fact, it cannot even,
on its own, die, for, as Traherne writes in a Biblical paraphrase,
"by himself it is that we come unto him . . . Thus are we in
Christ restored to the Exercise of that Power which we lost by
Sin: but without him we can do Nothing" (*CE*, pp. 66, 102; cf.
John 15:5). So restored, one sees, as God's Eye saw before the
Fall, that the whole universe is "very good" (Gen. 1:31). By
means of the Redemption, the psyche, would-be usurping pretender, learns and assumes its proper subordinate place; one sees
through the convention, and it also becomes a blessing. In other
words, we come closer to the essential Traherne by speaking not
of his easy optimism or failure to have a deep consciousness of sin
and evil but rather, far more accurately, of his sure and profound
realization of the nearness of God, whose "Essence is all Act"
("The Anticipation," p. 162) just as "My Spirit" is "all Act" (p.
52).

As to what, more particularly, pneuma or Spirit is, one must
begin by saying, "when you ask, I do not know; but when you
do not, I know." Because it is infinite, without *fin,* the true Self,

figured as a circle whose center is everywhere and whose circumference is nowhere, cannot be circumscribed or de*fin*ed.

> But being Simple like the Deitie
> In its own Centre is a Sphere
> Not shut up here, but evry Where.
>
> ("My Spirit," p. 50)

It will not sit for its photograph, cannot be reduced to what is flat, two-dimensional, unliving. It cannot be known intellectually because it is that which does the knowing, better described (if described at all) as an act or process rather than as a thing. According to the ancient Cabalists, the Godhead, uncreated deity, is *Ain Soph,* without end, incorporeal, nameless and unnameable, transcending entirely all human conception: exactly "No-thing." This is God as he is in himself, impersonal and ineffable, as distinct from the God of the Torah, who is God in manifestation.

Pico della Mirandola, whom we know Traherne read, had brought the Cabala into wider repute, but Traherne need not have learned directly from the Cabala, for this idea also abounds in Christian contemplative literature. St. Augustine, St. Bonaventura, and Nicolas Cusanus, for example, all know that crude images of God must be abandoned, for if one is to go beyond metaphor, they hold, one can only speak of God in negative terms. St. Thomas Aquinas expresses the idea succinctly and precisely: "in matters of Divinity, negative statements are to be preferred to positive, an account of our insufficiency, as Dionysius says." And that most famous traveler of the *via negativa,* Dionysius the pseudo-Areopagite, expounds the doctrine of Unknowing, of moving toward the Divine Darkness by denying all predicates of Him, for He is beyond the pale of predicating conceptualization. Or, putting it another way, ultimate Reality at last becomes so near as to sweep away the intellectual distinction between us and It. Eckhart, who variously refers to the Godhead as a "void as if he were not," "the wordless Godhead," "the nameless Nothing," "the still wilderness," teaches that we should "love him as he is: a not-God, a not-spirit, a not-Person, a not-image," for as "St. Bernard says: He who would know thee, God, must mete thee with no measure." Ruysbroeck speaks of "the abysmal Wayless-ness of God . . . so dark and so unconditioned," "the abyss of the Ineffable," "the dark silence in which all lovers lose them-selves." "When I consider what God is," Boehme writes, "I say: He is the One, face to face with the creature, that is, an eternal Nothing." Explaining the goal of the contemplative, the Blessed Henry Suso, who also describes the Godhead as an "unfathom-able abyss," instructs with this paradox: "by common agreement, men call this Nothing 'God', and it is itself a most essential Something. And here man knows himself to be one with this Nothing, and this Nothing knows itself without the action of the intellect . . . But whatever can be said of the Nothing by no means explains what it is, although there were as many doctors and books again." [17] When Traherne, who surely knew at least some of these Christian writers and who uses some of their lan-guage, exults "O what a Wonderful Profound Abyss is God!" ("The Anticipation," p. 161) and asserts that "the Soul [pneuma] is a Miraculous Abyss of infinit Abysses" (*C* II 83) and even when he "tautologically" exclaims that "A Sight of Happiness is Happiness" (*C* III 60), he is writing from within the tradition of negative theology; he is traveling the *via negativa*.[18]

All of this is to say that the Godhead is unknowable to the conceptual intellect (the center of the psyche), which functions by means of separation, discrimination, and analysis; its territory is *natura naturata,* that is, nature classified, sorted, murdered for dissection into "things," according to the faculties of the mind.

Indeed, as Kant held, time, space, and the categories of understanding are formal features of the mind or ego. Hence the phenomenal order (reality as we ordinarily, conventionally, perceive it) depends on the forms or structure of our minds. And hence, the mind prescribes its laws to nature rather than perceives nature as it is, *natura naturans,* "nature naturing," nature spontaneous and living. Kant's categories and the forms of time and space are not only a priori conditions to fallen experience but also inhibitors of full or redeemed experience. Holding, then, that the deity is intellectually incomprehensible, Christian mystics have believed, as a fundamental article of faith, that the true hierophant of the mysteries of God is love. By love may he be known; by love especially does man progress from egohood to Selfhood. As Traherne affirms, "By lov alone is GOD Enjoyed By Lov alone Delighted in" (*C* I 71). Thus one must become like unto a child, in whom conceptual powers are undeveloped and who gives himself wholly, selflessly, and thus "lovingly," to his present activity. Or, more precisely, since such becoming is not literal, "all our Thoughts must be Infant-like and Clear" (*C* III 5); the intellectual mode must not be the exclusive mode of knowing; the highest knowledge, the deepest vision embraces knowing by intuition or imagination or contemplation, which is a creative or re-creative act of love, of clearly seeing that even a grain of *"Sand is Endless . . . And every Thing is truly Infinite"* (CE, p. 181). Becoming like unto a child is recovering unified, whole, and holy vision.

But if the *via negativa* means essentially that the Godhead, the Eternal Source of all existence, is not intellectually knowable and is therefore ineffable, Christian mystics have also journeyed on the *via positiva;* that is, they have attempted to describe God, to evoke in us some notion of the divine nature. The distinction is often made between the predicateless Godhead and the personal God who has attributes. The negative way does not invalidate human thinking about God. Mental concepts of God verbalized in positive propositions are of their nature inadequate, but they are not worthless; they help at least to focus our minds at the level of rational thought. Traherne's older, great contemporary John Milton, who was not a mystic, similarly understood all of this, as *The Christian Doctrine* (I, ii) makes apparent. The positive descriptions, some philosophers and theologians contend, cannot be literal, but must be symbolic.[19] And we shall see in the following chapters that Traherne also employs a specialized symbolism in his poetry, the primary object of which is to teach man that he is indeed "God's son" and to make him profoundly realize what and how much that title means.

The doctrine of the Golden Mean, closely related to the theme of childhood, to the psyche-pneuma distinction, and to questions of good and evil, occupies a central place in Traherne's philosophy. Growing out of the first chapter of Genesis and perhaps also stemming from Aristotelian ethics, metaphysics, and terminology ("Golden Mean" in Traherne pertains to God's moderation or temperance, "that which perfecteth and blesseth the Creation" — *CE,* p. 183), the doctrine is, however, not primarily an ethical one but rather the metaphysical or cosmological view that, rightly apprehended, the "finite," natural world (including man), as it is, is excellent, perfect, "That infinit Worth shut up in the Limits of a Material Being, is the only way to a Real Infinity" (*C* III 20).[20] Traherne the Neoplatonist, who made extracts from Ficino's *Argumenta* and Latin translation of the *Republic* (British Museum MS. Burney 126), would have known that the lengthy, elaborate process of education described in Plato's *Republic* leads ideally to insight into the harmonious order of the whole world. As a Christian, he surely seems influenced by St. Augustine's and St. Thomas Aquinas' theological position that evil *non est substantia;* theirs is essentially a monistic theory of substance and goodness as interchangeable, evil being understood as a privation of good, as nonbeing. Similar philosophical positions were held by continental contemporaries of Traherne. For Spinoza, *omnis existentia est perfectio;* for Leibniz, the Pythagorean-Platonic theory of the harmony of the universe remained the abiding and basic principle of all his efforts to contruct a world view. Finally, the idea, as Whitman in "Starting from Paumanok" puts it, "that all of the things of the universe are perfect miracles" is recurrent among poet-mystics and expressive of one vital aspect of their actual mystical experiences. Traherne's doctrine of the Golden Mean, then, must not be facilely misconstrued as naive or Panglossian optimism, though it may seem so to those who do not trouble to try to understand it.

Traherne was very well aware that "there are many Disorders and Evils in the World, many Deformities, Sins and Miseries," and "It is not through Ignorance, or want of good Will that we speak [in *Christian Ethicks*] nothing of Vices, the woeful deformity of which being exposed to view, near the excellence of Vertue, would put a greater lustre on all their brightness: but the abundance of matter which Vertue itself doth afford, forbids us to waste our Time and Paper in the description of their Contraries . . . And besides this, the mischief and inconveniency of every Vice is so great and manifold that it would require a distinct and entire Volume to unfold the deformity of their destructive nature, so fully as their baseness and demerit requires" (*CE,* pp. 53, 206–207; and see pp. 3–4).

Although Traherne unquestionably knew profoundly, as the above quotations testify, that much evil exists in the world, he also understood, as Milton's Satan does not, that evil is nonbeing, nonfulfillment, that it is finally self-destructive, a futile effort at Self-negation. The de-emphasis on evil in his work stems from a deliberate choice of strategy, not from ignorance or easy optimism. An important part of that strategy lies in promulgating the doctrine of the Golden Mean, the perfection of Nature as it actually and ideally is in the unfallen and regenerated states. Through his subsuming theme of childhood in the Dobell poems, Traherne insists upon the everyday and every-moment validity and significance of the great biblical myth of the Creation and the Garden, which culminates in the Gospel story of Redemption. He affirms its historic and especially its individual and immediate validity and significance. For Traherne, a Christian in the fullest sense, the pattern of Creation-Fall-Redemption is literally true for all time, mythically or allegorically true for every individual as he passes in this life from childhood to adulthood to (all too rarely) sainthood, and eternally operative in every Now-moment.[21] Mythically, the newly born child, dwelling in the Edenic natural world, is, to begin with, wholly Good — in the sense of pre-moral and pre-intellectual, without knowledge of moral good and evil and without a developed, conceptualizing, reductively analytical psyche. In developing a psyche or ego, in growing up, men fall from original Goodness and a unified vision of the created world's perfection; and they need to recover that Goodness or God-likeness and a comparable vision. But, as we have seen, Traherne believes that the fallen psyche, without Christ or pneuma, can do nothing. Hence Traherne, whose views on Original Sin may appear unorthodox and Pelagian, is not to be finally regarded as Pelagian. Pelagius questioned the need of divine grace for man's salvation and thereby tended to render Christ's Crucifixion meaningless. Traherne, on the contrary, affirms that Christ overcomes, redeems, the "psychic" man.

The Goodness or perfection of God's created universe seems to be understood by Traherne primarily in aesthetic terms, but terms which nevertheless subsume moral good and evil. (This may be taken as a Neoplatonic element in Traherne's Christianity; but, then, in Genesis the account of the "very good" Creation *precedes* the story of the Fall, of acquiring knowledge of good and evil.) For right apprehension or vision does help lead one to the state of blessedness. Thus Traherne counsels: "above all, pray to be sensible of the Excellency of the Creation, for upon the due sense of its Excellency the life of Felicity wholly dependeth" (*CE,* p. 6). The redeemed man, who through Christ has sought and found, rediscovered, the kingdom of Heaven, will see "the Excellency of the Creation," will have transcended good and evil (he is post-moral and post-intellectual, so to speak, as the child is pre-moral and pre-intellectual), and will love and do as "he" wills. To be redeemed means to will not as the psyche does but as God, pneuma, does.

In a brilliant passage from the *Centuries,* Traherne expresses and implies much that we have been trying to clarify:

This visible World is Wonderfully to be Delighted in and Highly to be Esteemed, becaus it is the Theatre of GODS Righteous Kingdom. Who as Himself was Righteous becaus He made it freely, so He made it that We might freely be Righteous too. For in the Kingdom of Glory it is impossible to fall. No man can sin that clearly seeth the Beauty of Gods face: Becaus no Man can sin against his own Happiness. that is, none can when he sees it Clearly willingly and Wittingly forsake it. Tempter, Temptation, Loss and Danger being all seen: but here we see His Face in a Glasse, and more Dimly behold our Happiness as in a Mirror: by faith therfore we are to live, and to sharpen our Ey that we may see his Glory, We are to be Studious and Intent in our Desires and Endeavors. For we may sin, or we may be Holy. Holiness therfore and Righteousness naturally flow out of our fruition of the World: For who can vilify and debase Himself by any Sin, while he Actually considers he is the Heir of it? It exalts a Man to a Sublime and Honorable life: it lifts him abov Lusts and Makes Him Angelical. (II 97)

The seeming contradiction of condemning and enjoying the world Traherne resolves by arguing that there are two worlds: the perfect, natural world, including creatures and objects, and eternally created by God and by God in the redeemed man — indeed, the "visible World is the Body of God" (*C* II 21) — a glorious world for which, in Hebraic-Christian tradition, one renders joyful praise; and the fallen world fabricated by man's conceptualizing ego — an artificial, prideful, and ultimately illusory world, of which one should be contemptuous (the familiar but often misinterpreted theme of *contemptus mundi*). A passage in *Christian Ethicks* makes this distinction clearly: "all the Evils that are now in the world, men brought on themselves by the Fall: And there is great need of distinguishing between the works of GOD, and the works of men. For all that GOD did is Lovely and Divine: nothing is bitter and distasteful, but what we have done: himself surveyed the whole Creation, and pronounced concerning every Thing, that it *was exceeding Good*" (pp. 53–54; see also *C* I 7). Such a traditional religious distinction has of course Platonic parallels, but Traherne was perhaps enough of an Aristotelian and certainly enough of an enlightened Christian so as not to share any Platonic disparagement of the visible world. He spends considerable effort in the *Meditations on the Six Days of the Creation,* the *Thanksgivings,* the *Centuries,* and *Christian Ethicks* discussing and trying to establish the doctrine of the Golden Mean,[22] and this doctrine underlies and informs the poems. "This glorious Light must needs be a most blessed Thing," Traherne writes in *Meditations on the Six Days of the Creation,* "For God himself beholding it, said, *it was very good*" (p. 13). While revealing who we really are, God's sons, the poems should at the same time help us to see with a redeemed Eye that God's whole universe truly is "very good.

Two. Traherne's Poetic: Mode out of Vision and Tradition

All Tropes are Clouds; Truth doth it self excel,
Whatever Heights, Hyperboles can tell.

Thanksgivings

GIVEN THE GREAT INFLUENCE OF THE Bible on Western literature, it should not be surprising to find the fundamental biblical pattern of Creation-Fall-Redemption in many literary works which attempt to express some kind of total vision or world-view. Works by Dante, Spenser, Milton, Blake, and Wordsworth, for example, come readily to mind. Since each writer's treatment differs, a critic's special contribution would seem to lie in discussing and revealing the individuation — the distinctive themes, symbols, metaphors, and so forth — which a particular writer gives to the overriding archetype. In the preceding chapter, we have tried generally to locate Traherne in his proper context: Christian biblical, mystical tradition and, in particular, its fundamental myth. And we have discussed several key ideas shared by Traherne and Christian contemplatives especially for the light that these ideas will shed on Thomas Traherne's poetry. In this and the remaining chapters, we shall be directly concerned with that poetry and with what is distinctive in it, as we develop and demonstrate the general thesis that not only Traherne's thought but his poetic theory and practice as well may best be understood from the perspective of Christian mysticism.

This present chapter primarily concerns Traherne's poetic theory and its growth out of his own mystical vision and the confirming biblical, contemplative tradition which underlies his work. By learning something of his poetic, we will not only further establish and reveal his mysticism but will also acquire additional valuable insight into his poetic practice. Although a detailed examination of the Dobell Folio poems awaits the discussion of Chapters 3-5, as we consider Traherne's poetic theory in this chapter we shall naturally also have in mind and often touch and dwell upon his actual practice.

Traherne's statement of his poetic is found most fully in "The Author to the Critical Peruser" (pp. 2-3) and incidentally here

35

and there throughout his writings. Unfortunately, "The Author to the Critical Peruser" exists only as edited by Philip. But as it deals more with aesthetic than moral matters, Philip probably did not feel impelled to alter it to the same extent he generally did the other poems. Moreover, the incidental and indirect statements of poetic found in D poems and elsewhere substantiate its views. Also, internal evidence suggests that the poem should precede "The Salutation," which appears in the same relative position in both D and F. Whether "The Author to the Critical Peruser" would, by Thomas' choice, have preceded D or F or some combination of D and F poems, it was clearly to preface some one volume of Thomas' poems, and as its statement of purpose as well as of poetic is corroborated by D poems we perhaps may with some assurance regard it essentially as Thomas'. In any case, any theory of Traherne's poetic that we deduce from it and his other works will have to be further developed and substantiated in practice by the D poems themselves.

"The Author to the Critical Peruser" begins:

> The naked Truth in many faces shewn,
> Whose inward Beauties very few hav known,
> A Simple Light, transparent Words, a Strain
> That lowly creeps, yet maketh Mountains plain,
> Brings down the highest Mysteries to sense
> And keeps them there; that is Our Excellence:
> At that we aim; to th' end thy Soul might see
> With open Eys thy Great *Felicity,*
> Its Objects view, and trace the glorious Way
> Wherby thou may'st thy Highest Bliss enjoy.
>
> No curling Metaphors that gild the Sence,
> Nor Pictures here, nor painted Eloquence.   (p. 2)

To see the noumenal — or better, numinous — in the phenomenal
is Traherne's object. Ordinary language by its very nature, by the
subject-object dualism upon which it is constructed, distinguishes
and divides (sometimes usefully enough) into two what is for
the contemplatives nondual. It is not even so much that the infinite is in the finite as that the two are one and yet, paradoxically,
are distinct: they are abstractly distinguishable but not actually
divisible. Thus Traherne must find a "language," a mode of expression, which transcends conventional notions and notations and
reveals that, rightly apprehended, the light of day is eternal, the
grain of sand endless. And this is to be done "to th' end thy Soul
might see With open Eys thy Great *Felicity*." As indicated generally by all his major writings, a central intention of Traherne
was to direct other men to that Happiness which is Blessedness,
his own greater Felicity being largely consequent upon theirs. The
last poem of the Folio, "Goodnesse," begins, we recall, "The Bliss
of other Men is my Delight" (p. 182). The Dobell sequence is itself a kind of microcosmic "Circulation": Traherne apparently intended to communicate his bliss for the bliss of other men, which
in turn would have given him further joy. Who can read his poetry without responding to the essential joy, in the reading and
perhaps also in subsequent experiences? [1] In a special sense, the
two traditional values of poetry, truth and pleasure, are correlative
and interdependent in Traherne's poetry: his poetry is joyfully to
show "The naked Truth," to instruct truthfully in pleasure, happiness, "thy Highest Bliss."

Like George Herbert,[2] Traherne would exclude from his poetry
"curling Metaphors that gild the Sence"; there are to be no "Pictures here, nor painted Eloquence." This cannot mean, as similarly
it did not for Herbert, that there is to be no metaphor at all; for in
this same poem and variously throughout his poetry Traherne does
in fact express himself in metaphor, sometimes in extended meta-

phor. Emphasis must fall on "curling." Traherne may mean that he will avoid not only (as the subsequent lines 21–30 indicate) aureate diction, classical imitation, and obscure allusion (Margoliouth, II, 336) but also certain kinds of metaphor, perhaps the metaphysical conceit in its more extreme forms; that is, not the conceit or metaphor which truly unites but those metaphors which yoke violently together extreme dissimilars. His poetic practice bears this assumption out. In this respect, Traherne may be regarded as a transitional figure, eschewing or minimizing aureate diction, classical imitation and obscure allusion, as generally the Metaphysical poets do, but nevertheless looking forward to the next literary period, with its Johnsonian censuring of the hyperbolic conceit.

Yet Traherne means much more than that. It is also more than a matter of sometimes appropriately expressing the theme of childhood by means of childlike, literal language. The second half of "The Author to the Critical Peruser" (ll. 37–64), like "The Person," indicates that for Traherne, as for Blake, "Art can never exist without Naked Beauty displayed" (*Laocoon*). Traherne apparently intends to use language "literally" as a means of direct pointing to "The Naked Truth," to the perfection of God's universe as it is. Style must be an echo to the sense. A naked style is effective for showing the naked truth, awakening and cleansing man's perceptual and imaginative powers, "resurrecting" the human body, and revealing "God's Work" and

> the *Soul,* in whose concealed [3] Face,
> Which comprehendeth all unbounded Space,
> God may be seen.   (p. 3)

Thus in many poems Traherne uses the "literal catalog" for direct pointing, as in "Speed":

The World my House, the Creatures were my Goods,
    Fields, Mountains, Valleys, Woods,
Floods, Cities, Churches, Men, for me did shine.   (p. 68)

This poetic receives corroboration in the second stanza of "The Person":

                The Naked Things
            Are most Sublime, and Brightest shew
                When they alone are seen:
            Mens Hands then Angels Wings
            Are truer Wealth even here below:
                For those but seem.
        Their Worth they then do best reveal,
            When we all Metaphores remove,
                For Metaphores conceal,
                And only Vapours prove.
        They best are Blazond when we see
                The Anatomie,
        Survey the Skin, cut up the Flesh, the Veins
            Unfold: The Glory there remains.
        The Muscles, Fibres, Arteries and Bones
        Are better far then Crowns and precious Stones.   (p. 76)

Considering "Angel Wings," Traherne's disapproval of curling metaphors would seem to include encrusted religious language which has lost its original meaning and so is taken to refer only to a God remotely located somewhere in the distant skies rather than immanent or only to a future Happy Place after death rather than to the here and now after the "death" of the ego. In this connection, one may well ponder the realistic good sense that Traherne displays in *C* IV 9.

"No curling Metaphors," then, reflects Traherne's intention to use language in some way literally, and often in catalogs, in order to point directly to the naked Reality, the eternity which is here and now. He wishes us to see

> His Glory here on Earth to be Divine,
> And that his GODHEAD in his Works doth shine.
>
> ("The Enquirie," p. 84)

For "His Throne is neer, tis just before our face" ("Thoughts IV," p. 181). By the mode of the bare catalog of words used recurrently and literally — a style of essences — Traherne hopes we will grasp without mediation, or with the least mediation, the Reality which is "just before our face." Such a poetic practice, similar to Whitman's, is also comparable, I think, to certain direct methods of Zen Buddhism for attaining *satori,* enlightenment. When the monk asks the master "what is the Buddha [ultimate reality]?" the master may reply simply "three pounds of flax!" or he may strike the monk on the head — an answer we may perhaps think of as the oriental *via negativa.* To the question, Traherne replies simply, "Fields, Mountains, Valleys, Woods." "When it sees a mountain," D. T. Suzuki writes in reference to Zen, "it declares it to be a mountain; when it comes to a river, it just tells us it is a river." [4] And consider how much this haiku sounds like Traherne:

> How wondrously supernatural,
> And how miraculous, this!
> I draw water, and I carry fuel! [5]

How can you make someone really understand and see the naked truth — incomprehensible to the intellect — that the uncorrupted natural world, even the simplest act, is perfect, holy, divine? By hitting, surprise, exclamation, direct pointing, no curling metaphors, the barest catalogs. The form is adapted to the content; or better, content finds its suitable, inevitable form.

This deliberate, purposeful practice of using words literally, especially certain recurrent words and especially in catalogs, is no doubt a major reason why critics have felt Traherne's poetry to be "prosy," while failing to see that this use, this mode of expression, is inherent to and arises ineluctably out of Traherne's meaning and intention. I would agree that Traherne's poetry is "prosy," that his true medium is prose, not poetry, if the literal, cataloging mode were the only characteristic of his poetry. But it is not. There are other distinctly poetic qualities in his poetry — also intimately connected to meaning, not merely decorative — such as rhythm, imagery, symbol, complexity and variety of stanzaic pattern, economy of expression, and exact, reflexive, and paradoxical use of language. These qualities will constitute a main concern of all our subsequent discussion.

Another, still more fundamental reason why Traherne chooses to "remove metaphors," will have "No curling Metaphors," "Nor Pictures," is that he knows with the mystics of the *via negativa* that the highest truth is imageless and unknowable to the conceptual intellect and that therefore one must somehow go beyond metaphor:

> All Tropes are Clouds; Truth doth it self excel,
> Whatever Heights, Hyperboles can tell.
>
> (p. 223; see *C* II 52)

These lines from the *Thanksgivings* are not intended as a denunciation and disavowal of metaphor. Indeed, they employ metaphor, and the very next line implies Traherne's great admiration for divine poetry: "O that I were as *David,* the sweet Singer of *Israel!*" The lines, rather, express the view that though tropes and hyperboles can reach certain poetic heights of insight the whole and highest truth is always superior to and other than all verbal efforts at portraying it. One sees here a Platonic and particularly Augustinian emphasis.[6] In addition to his other characterizing distinctions, the mystic is precisely he who profoundly realizes that a vast distance obtains between language and Reality and so does not make the mistake, as others consciously or unconsciously do, of identifying Reality with either plain, literal statement or metaphorical expression. And Traherne's poetic is apparently based upon that realization.

To the question in what way is one to apprehend God, Eckhart answers, "Thou shalt know him without semblance and without means." Similarly, St. Edmund Rich, speaking of three forms of contemplation, the third and highest being an infused contemplation which leads along the *via negativa,* instructs in this manner: "put every corporeal image outside your heart, and let your naked intention fly up above all human reasoning, and there you shall find such great sweetness and such great secrets that without special grace there is no-one who can think of it except only him who has experienced it."[7] The mystic experience, which cannot be attained by words alone, neither reading, writing, nor incanting them, is itself ineffable. Yet mystics do choose to write of and about it. Traherne, who affirms that God's "Greatest Gifts . . . are unattainable by Book" (*C* III 1), still goes on writing a book. And in their writing the mystics use, as Traherne does, metaphors, images. How, then, can a poet-mystic reconcile the mystic wisdom and necessity of silence, the coming to "know him without semblance and without means," with the desire to help impart that wisdom to others?

Traditionally, there are many ways. And Traherne seems to

have developed from certain traditional biblical, mystical terminology his own distinctive way. What is remarkable and here
pertinent about Traherne's images is that they tend to be concentrated and tend to occur within catalogs of other concentrated
images. By "concentrated image" I mean an image which passes
from metaphoric into symbolic values. It gathers and focuses
meanings — as the mirrors of a microscope concentrate the light
upon the slide — meanings which are central and vital to the poem;
or, to change our own metaphor, the concentrated image explored
is an atom exploded: it releases stored energies; it is a sunburst of
multiple meaning. It does not rest with the immediate image
evoked but turns the imagination back upon the historical poetic
and religious meanings of the word or phrase. Part of the answer,
then, to the preceding question lies in Traherne's symbolism. For,
as Carlyle writes, "in a Symbol there is concealment and yet
revelation: here therefore, by Silence and by Speech acting together, comes a double significance . . . In the Symbol proper,
what we can call a Symbol, there is ever, more or less distinctly
and directly, some embodiment and revelation of the Infinite; the
Infinite is made to blend itself with the Finite, to stand visible,
and as it were, attainable there." [8] Traherne's poetry is often most
effective when two of his main poetic characteristics combine,
when there is a catalog of concentrated images or symbols. And it
strikes me that this extremely economical poetic mode of recurrent
catalogs of symbols is as perfect a reconciliation of the *via negativa*
and *via positiva* as might possibly be effected in poetry.

Abjuring *curling* metaphors, then, Traherne also means to use
concentrated images. His metaphors tend to become symbols. The
symbol is more useful and appropriate for Traherne in that,
whereas the metaphor maintains the distinction between its primary and secondary terms, the symbol, as Paul Tillich says, "participates in the power of that which it symbolizes." [9] In the Dobell

Folio, several related groups of frequently recurring symbols seem rather directly suited to the theme of childhood because they serve admirably to reveal who man truly is, what his essential nature is, and wherein his Felicity lies. They are therefore what we may designate as "pneuma-revealing" symbols. Traherne characteristically chooses words and images that are designed by tradition and his own unique employment of them to enlighten and convince us that man's essential self is pneuma rather than psyche and to give us some intuition of the nature of that Self. He uses many of these key words or image clusters in a symbolic way in some contexts and literally in other contexts, sometimes both literally and symbolically in the same poem. The literal and symbolic meanings are played off against one another, as we shall see, for example, in "Desire."

Traherne's use of recurrent words is varied yet consistent enough for regular patterns to be discerned so that we can distinguish seven major groups or classes of pneuma-revealing symbols. Though there are several related words or symbols in each group, one word may serve to denominate each group: (1) Eye, (2) Sphere, (3) Sun, (4) Mirror, (5) King, (6) Dwelling Place, (7) Fountain. There are also other, less frequently recurring words sometimes used symbolically, such as abyss, angel, bride, friend, vine.

This traditional symbolism is so deeply assimilated by Traherne, so widely characteristic of him, that one finds it not only in the poetry but also, in varying degrees, throughout the "Select Meditations," "Church's Year-Book," *Meditations on the Six Days of the Creation, Thanksgivings, Centuries,* and *Christian Ethicks.* For example, the *Meditations on the Six Days of the Creation* employs the Sun and Fountain symbolism most extensively, that of the Mirror and Dwelling Place or Temple somewhat less so; and in the *Thanksgivings for the Soul* symbols from all seven major groups, as one might expect, appear repeatedly. In the Dobell Folio, at least one and usually more of either these symbols or the "symbol words" used in a literal, nonsymbolic sense (and often both) occur in every poem except the fragmentary, seven-line "The Apprehension." The first three groups certainly, and possibly the fourth, are both imagistically similar enough and traditionally interrelated so that we may discuss them together; we shall then treat the last three groups separately.

Since Felicity is so much a matter of right apprehension, it should be no surprise that of all these symbols, the word eye (or Ey) is the most frequent, occurring, often symbolically, at least forty-six times in the thirty-seven poems of the Dobell Folio. Under the Eye group, one includes the related and also frequent "Sight." Thus in "My Spirit" (p. 50), a poem which Margoliouth regards as Traherne's most comprehensive, Traherne refers to Spirit as "my Sight" and as a "Living Orb of Sight." The word Orb, occurring only in the very symbolic "The Preparative" and "My Spirit," may, by meaning and imagery, serve as a transition or link between the symbols Eye and Sphere, the latter word appearing some seventeen times in the Dobell Folio. To continue to illustrate from the same poem, Traherne paradoxically describes "my Spirit" both positively as "a Sphere Not shut up here, but evry Where," "A Strange Mysterious Sphere" and, twice in stanza 6, negatively as "not a Sphere"; and immediately in the next stanza he again apostrophizes, "O Sphere of Light, O Sphere of Joy." Logically minded critics may fancy that Traherne had difficulty with this poem[10] when actually he is by paradox travel-ing both the *via positiva* and the *via negativa*. The whole truth can be hinted at only by paradox, by both affirmation and denial, as when Eckhart writes: "I have said that there is one agent alone in the soul that is free. Sometimes I have called it the tabernacle of the Spirit. Other times I have called it the Light of the Spirit and again, a spark. Now I say that it is neither this nor that."[11] Traherne's thought and mode of expression is paradoxical in a fundamental, pervasive, and organic way (rather than, say, in the manner of frequent witty or startling lines, though there are occasional such lines in Traherne) because mystical experience itself is basically and characteristically paradoxical.[12]

The third group of symbols, by imagery and meaning related to the first two, includes the words Sun, Light, and Fire and, secondarily, Beam, Ray, Day, and the important Shine. Fire and light imagery pervades the Folio. By frequency of occurrence alone this group is also an extremely significant one. Only once, in "Fullnesse" (p. 58), does Traherne employ the word Spark: "A little Spark . . . shining in the Dark." More often, he uses the analogous Image or Glass and Mirror, our fourth group. The appositive and ecstatic second stanza of "The Preparative" contains a number of these major symbols:

> Then was my Soul my only All to me,
>   A Living Endless Ey,
>   Far wider than the Skie
> Whose Power, whose Act, whose Essence was to see.
>   I was an Inward *Sphere of Light,*
> Or an Interminable Orb of *Sight,*
>   An Endless and a Living Day,
> *A vital Sun* that round about did *ray*
>   All Life and Sence,
> A Naked Simple Pure *Intelligence.*   (p. 20)

These images and phrases are traditional symbols of Neoplatonic philosophy as well as of Christianity. Familiar enough to us, they were even more familiar to the seventeenth-century man. He would know fire has always been associated with divinity, with the appearance of God to Moses, Isaiah, Ezekiel, and St. John; in his Bible he would read of the Old Testament God who "is a consuming fire" (Deut. 4:24), of Christ who "shall baptize you with the Holy Ghost, and with fire" and who "will burn up the chaff with unquenchable fire" (Matt. 3:11–12), and of the Holy Ghost who appeared to the Apostles as "tongues . . . of fire" (Acts 2:3). In Boehme's works, translated into English between 1645 and 1662, he might read a paradoxical passage such as this: "we are able then to recognize that the eternal Unground out of Nature is a will, like an eye wherein Nature is hidden; like a hidden fire that burns not, which exists and also exists not. It is not a spirit, but a form of spirit, like the reflection in the mirror." [13] Among the English mystics, he would read — the titles themselves being pertinent — St. Aelred of Rievaulx's *The Mirror of Love* or Richard Rolle's *Incendium Amoris*. When he went into his church he would see above a high altar a picture of the all-seeing eye, representing the deity in all its power and majesty, or he would gaze upon a nimbus, a symbol of divine power and undoubtedly a Christianized form of the solar disc; the sphere or circle would be recognized as symbolic of God and of eternity. In his reading of emblem books he would come upon a print depicting a devout suppliant kneeling with an arrow leading from his breast and pointing upward toward the eye of God. The frequent Son-sun pun would appear in the seventeenth-century man's reading of poets, as in Donne's "Sweare by thy selfe, that at my death thy Sunne Shall shine as it shines now." He would notice it too in his reading of the Bible — "the Sun of righteousness [shall] arise with healing in his wings" (Malachi 4:2) — as he would the many references to Christ as the light or the Morning Star. He would know well that in the Christian tradition the sun is a figure "of the *central point, the Eternal Now* in which man's consciousness must come to rest if he is to be liberated from time." [14]

The last three major classes of Traherne's symbolism — King, Dwelling Place, Fountain — are, like the first four, traditional symbols of the Godhead, God, and God-like element in man; and, because they too are found pervasively in the Bible and in contemplative literature, they impart a resonant and subtle power to Traherne's poetry. The Psalms, especially, repeatedly use the King symbolism: as Herbert was later to conclude "Jordan I," the Psalms plainly, appositively, say "my God, my King" (68:24). And of course the New Testament frequently refers to Christ as "the King that cometh in the name of the Lord," "the King of the Jews" (Luke 19:38; 23:3) and "the King of kings, and Lord of lords" (1 Tim. 6:15). Writing of Christ's kingship, Julian of Norwich employs the crown image with this pertinence: "the Son . . . stands directly before His Father, richly clad in joyful splendour, with a rich and precious crown upon his head. For it was revealed that we are His crown, and this crown is the Father's joy, the Son's honour, the Holy Spirit's delight, and the endless and wonderful bliss of all who are in heaven." [15] The King symbolism obtains also in such related words as throne, regal, treasures, diadem, and so forth, as well as crown. Often Traherne juxtaposes, combines, or fuses symbols from several major groups, thereby achieving compounded, intense effects. Thus, men's "Eys" are "the Thornes, their Hearts the Heavnly Rooms, Their Souls the Diadems" ("The Enquirie," p. 84). In the still greater complexity of the first stanza of "The Person" one has the pleasure of following the extended development of a metaphor as well as "seeing" the body resurrected by means of Traherne's King symbolism:

Ye Sacred Lims,
A richer Blazon I will lay
  On you, then first I found:
  That like Celestial Kings,
Ye might with Ornaments of Joy
  Be always Crownd.
A Deep Vermilion on a Red,
  On that a Scarlet I will lay,
  With Gold Ile Crown your Head,
  Which like the Sun shall Ray.
  With Robes of Glory and Delight
  Ile make you Bright.
Mistake me not, I do not mean to bring
  New Robes, but to Display the Thing:
Nor Paint, nor Cloath, nor Crown, nor add a Ray,
But Glorify by taking all away.   (p. 74)

The symbolism of the Dwelling Place includes such related or synonymous words as temple, tabernacle, tower, fort, palace, court, house, rooms, and bower. The tabernacle (literally meaning tent) or temple (1 Sam. 1:9) is the dwelling place of God, the ark of the covenant or tabernacle being a symbol of God's presence with his people (Ex. 26:1; Heb. 9:2, 3). The Bible repeatedly refers to God as a tower (Ps. 61:3; Pr. 18:10; 2 Sam. 22: 3). And the temple is Christ's body or human nature, in which the Godhead dwells (John 2:19, 21), or it is the human body in which the Spirit of God dwells (1 Cor. 3:16). Moreover, "in my Father's house are many mansions" (John 14:2). This symbolism, central in George Herbert and frequent in the mystics, is perhaps most famous in the primary image of the *Interior Castle* of St. Teresa, who envisions "the soul as if it were a castle . . .

in which there are many rooms [*aposentos:* dwelling place, abode], just as in Heaven there are many mansions [*moradas:* derived from *morar,* to dwell]"; later in this same work, St. Teresa imagines "that God is like a very large and beautiful mansion or palace." Similarly, Dame Julian writes that "He made man's soul to be His own city and His dwelling place, which is the most pleasing to Him of all His works." [16] In "The Meditations on the Sixth Day's Creation," Traherne compares man at length to a temple and, quoting Lactantius, provides this gloss: "The Temple of God . . . is not *Lime, Stone, Sand, and Timber, but Man bearing the Image of God. And this Temple is not adorn'd with Gold or Silver, but with divine Virtues and Graces*" (p. 75). Throughout Traherne's poems, man and nature are "the Godheads Dwelling Place" ("The Vision," p. 26). In "Thoughts IV," "The Soul . . . sees The New Jerusalem, the Palaces . . . of the DEITIE" (p. 180). "My Spirit" is the "Temple of his Whole Infinitie" (p. 56).

> It is my Davids Tower
> Where all my Armor lies.   ("Fullnesse," p. 58)

As with the King symbolism, this group in Traherne may have been particularly influenced by David, his favorite: in "Thoughts II," Traherne affirms that the

> Temple David did intend,
> Was but a Thought, and yet it did transcend
> King Solomons.   (p. 173)

The seventh or Fountain group includes the related Springs, Streams, Ocean.[17] Water imagery, related to images of growth, of flowers and fruits, is very frequent in the Dobell Folio and also has special symbolic significance. Alluding to the well-known biblical passage which refers to "the Lord" as "the fountain of living waters" (Jer. 17:13) and characteristically interweaving several of his major symbols, Traherne writes of God's works, which are "Thoughts" (IV), that

> All these are in his Omnipresence still
> As Living Waters from his Throne they trill.
> As Tokens of his Lov they all flow down,
> Their Beauty Use and Worth the Soul do Crown . . .
>
> His Dwelling place is full of Joys and Pleasures,
> His Throne a fountain of Eternal Treasures.　　　(p. 181)

Teaching that all things are emanations from God, an inevitable overflow of his infinite actuality, Plotinus employed not only the metaphor of the sun which radiates light without loss to itself but also the metaphor of the spring from which the stream flows without exhausting its infinite source. Apparently influenced by Plotinean terminology as well as thought, Traherne writes in "The Circulation":

> All things do first receiv, that giv.
> 　　Only tis GOD above,
> That from, and in himself doth live,
> 　　Whose All sufficient Love
> Without Original can flow
> And all the Joys and Glories shew
> Which Mortal Man can take Delight to know
> He is the Primitive Eternal Spring
> The Endless Ocean of each Glorious Thing.　　(p. 154)

The "Amendment" to this is epitomized in a series of rhetorical questions and pneuma-revealing symbols:

> Am I a Glorious Spring
> Of Joys and Riches to my King?
> Are Men made Gods! And may they see
> So Wonderful a Thing
> As GOD in me!
> And is my Soul a Mirror that must Shine
> Even like the Sun, and be far more Divine?[18]   (p. 156)

And, in an extended, interfused way, all of the last three groups are represented in the second stanza of "Love":

> Did not I covet to behold
> Som Endless Monarch, that did always live
> In Palaces of Gold
> Willing all Kingdoms Realms and Crowns to give
> Unto my Soul! Whose Lov
> A Spring might prov
> Of Endless Glories, Honors, friendships, Pleasures,
> Joys, Praises, Beauties and Celestial Treasures!
> Lo, now I see there's such a King,
> The fountain Head of evry Thing!   (p. 168)

It is as if the symbols are made to achieve among themselves what Traherne wishes man to achieve with God.

We have noticed but a few examples of Traherne's major symbolism and have seen them without the benefit of their sequential context and the enriching reflexive interplay of all the symbols. By their very nature and function, these symbols suggest more than any criticism can define. Criticism, which performs its analytic tasks to the end of its own eventual self-effacement and a new, more immediate, synthetic understanding of its literary object, must, unlike poetry, proceed in a discursive, step-by-step fashion. But in "following" the order of the D poems, as the remaining chapters do, we shall have opportunities to continue discussion of Traherne's symbols and to reveal more fully and clearly the connection between theory and practice, as well as to point out some of the other ordering, unifying links between the poems. A completely exhaustive account of the symbols and links is here neither possible nor necessary.

To recapitulate, Traherne characteristically writes in catalogs and appositions of recurrent traditional biblical and mystical terms used literally and symbolically. This is an economic and effective way of (1) promulgating the doctrine of the Golden Mean by directly pointing to "Eternity . . . in the Light of the Day" (*C* III 3) or in the fields, mountains, woods, and so forth, and by indicating the splendor and variety of the world and of every part, the infinite value of even the seemingly most insignificant, infinitesimal part; and (2) symbolizing and suggesting pneuma, teaching Self-knowledge, revealing who we really are. These two ends, difficult indeed to accomplish, both necessitate and are admirably served by Traherne's poetic and unifying device of various, repeated, special catalogs and appositions. Dobell was quite right, perhaps even more so than he knew, in his suggestion, which anticipated and partially answered the later critical charge of repetition, that Traherne is playing variations upon his favorite themes. But it is more than simply a matter of playing variations. In addition, many of the repetitions, including those which do not appear within catalogs or within appositions, are, as we shall see when we discuss the Dobell sequence in the following chapters, actually also essential stylistic and formal devices of coherence and unity. Above all — and beyond attempting variously to describe a complex truth that is very difficult to comprehend, a Truth "Whose inward Beauties very few hav known" — Traherne is trying, through his varied, ordered, interrelated repetitions and by other means, to help bring about, in Underhill's words, that "most actual, though indescribable phenomenon, the coming forth into consciousness of man's deeper, spiritual self," to help effect, in his own words, the Soul's seeing "With open Eys thy Great *Felicity*" and tracing "the glorious Way Wherby thou may'st thy Highest Bliss enjoy" (p. 2).

Furthermore, Traherne's poetry is "imitative" of the mystic experience in the sense that in the experience the mystic may simply be impelled to utter, exclaim, a word like "love," or "my God!" His poetry, often, at its best, most intense, attains by various poetic means to the stage wherein naming, cataloging in itself, is sufficient to convey a profound sense of the experience. The experience is so meaningful that no words in themselves can render it completely accurately or fully. Given such circumstances, the best poetry, like the best prayers, may well be the barest and most direct and also the most meaningfully symbolic. Only by some such specialized mode of expression can the poet-contemplative hope to make public and communicable his more private experiences in all their subtlety, vividness, and uniqueness. Though almost all poets use the catalog to some degree, perhaps it is no accident that the two poets who are especially distinguished for cataloging, Traherne and Whitman, are both mystics.

The possible influence on Traherne of seventeenth-century poetic theory and practice, which in general abjured and avoided merely ornamental or decorative language, and of developing seventeenth-century science's and philosophy's insistence on clear and distinct language and suspicion toward metaphoric language (from Bacon through Hobbes and Sprat) need not be excluded from any attempt to appreciate Traherne's poetic style.[19] But, given the primary concern of this chapter, a more fruitful way of regarding Traherne's style is to continue to see it shaped by his biblical, contemplative tradition and vision.

Apart from the traditional symbols we have just discussed, biblical quotations, paraphrases, echoes, and rhythms also resound throughout Traherne's works. The Bible's free system of versification unquestionably influenced the freely flowing parallelistic prose-poetry of the *Thanksgivings,* with its abundant appositions and cumulative catalogs, as it did also the comparable poetry of Blake and Whitman. Harold Fisch has remarked with respect to the *Thanksgivings* and *Centuries,* and he could have added the *Meditations on the Six Days of the Creation,* that "Traherne was perhaps of all the religious writers of the seventeenth century the most deeply conscious of the *Psalms* as a model for writing and as a model for the good life." [20] That deep consciousness obtains especially in the poetry. Like David, and George Herbert too, Traherne made of his heart's temple of religious thought a manifest poetic structure in the Dobell Folio sequence. We have seen that Traherne chooses biblical and other traditional images and symbols which turn the imagination back upon historical poetic and religious meanings. He puts these words into intense appositions and employs them variously and repeatedly throughout the sequence for increasingly magnified effects. His repetitive, accumulative, symbolic, and appositive style may well owe much to the Bible's frequent use of words which are central and emphasized in one passage and then picked up again elsewhere, thus establishing an unobtrusive cross reference — an association which, even if only dimly felt, adds dimension to the meaning. Herbert, who employed in *The Temple* the same biblical technique of repeated words, phrases, and images, specifies the method in "The H. Scriptures. II":

> This verse marks that, and both do make a motion
> Unto a third, that ten leaves off doth lie.

In addition to the effect of the Bible upon Traherne's poetry, both mystic traditions of the positive and negative ways appear to have shaped or to have significantly contributed to his style. Because the poet-mystic cannot remain silent, because he must find verbal expression to impart his experience and wisdom, Traherne's naked and appositive modes, his repeated literal and symbolic catalogs, his concentrated images, the tendency of his metaphors to become symbols, his fundamental, pervasive, and organic paradoxicality, the basic tension in his poetry between exuberance and restraint, plenitude and economy — all seem a perfect reconciliation of the *via positiva* and the *via negativa*. Repetition can be seen as an impulse stemming from the positive way; and the catalog, the concentrated image or symbol, and paradox appear as a balance struck between both ways. The *via negativa* finds expression also in some of the traditional language of negative theology — for example, "Abyss" in such poems as "The Salutation," "My Spirit," and "The Anticipation" — and in the overall movement in Traherne's work toward silence.

Remarking upon the solitary numeral II, which concludes the *Centuries* and stands at the head of a blank page in the manuscript, followed by 49 blank leaves, Louis Martz quite rightly indicates this movement in the *Centuries*:

> "In spite of this numerical heading for another section," Margoliouth has said (*1, 297*), "and in spite of Traherne's obvious idea of writing 'The fifth Centurie' I cannot but look on V. 10 as a triumphant and perfect conclusion. How could Traherne have gone beyond it? The *Centuries* are not unfinished." Another way of summing up this sense of comple-

tion would be to say that the conclusion lies in the eloquent silence of those blank pages, suggesting the "darkness of instructive silence" described by "Dionysius the Areopagite" in a quotation given by Bonaventure near the close of his seventh chapter: a darkness and silence "in which all is aglow, pouring out upon the invisible intellects the splendors of invisible goodness." Seen from this point of view, that solitary numeral, II, seems to reach out toward the silence of mystical repose.[21]

The reader of the poetry becomes more deeply aware of the value and significance of silence for the pre-verbal, unfallen child and the post-verbal, redeemed adult in poems like "The Preparative," "Dumnesse," and "Silence." And he should see that the "splendors of invisible goodness," revealed in the paradoxically illuminating darkness and silence that Dionysius and Bonaventure write of, obtain also in "Goodnesse," a poem with a truncated final stanza, the last poem of the Dobell Folio. In that poem, directly pointing particularly to the human face and symbolically suggesting pneuma, Traherne describes a Goodness that is at once both visible and invisible. "All our greatest philosophers and theologians unanimously assert that the visible universe is a faithful reflection of the invisible, and that from creatures we can rise to a knowledge of the Creator, 'in a mirror and in a dark manner,' as it were." [22] So writes Nicolas Cusanus, who must have had in mind, among others, St. Paul: "for the invisible things of him from the creation of the world are clearly seen, being understood by the things that are made, *even* his eternal power and Godhead" (Rom. 1:20). Traherne, I believe, would not have regarded such statements as mere commonplaces nor even only as kinds or bits of rational cosmological or teleological arguments for the existence of God, arguments which reason abstractly from the existence of visible things or visible design to the existence of an invisible Creator or Designer, in the manner, say, of Aquinas in the *Summa Theologica* (I, 2, 3). Rather, Traherne would also have taken these and the various similar statements to be found in biblical, contemplative literature ("all our greatest philosophers and theologians") as confirmations of his childhood and redeemed adult intuitions and right apprehensions. As the *Centuries* express it: "Eternity was Manifest in the Light of the Day, and som thing infinit Behind evry thing appeared" (III, 3; see also II, 17). That is, Traherne means actually experiencing the divine in visible things, directly perceiving the infinite in or within ("Behind") the finite. This experience is, precisely, one vital dimension of mysticism.

It is conventional and useful (though oversimplifying) to classify mystical experiences as being either "extrovertive," conveyed to the mystic through his physical senses, or "introvertive," reached by the *via negativa*. Traherne's catalogs, we have seen, point directly or suggest symbolically, and sometimes, as in "Desire," a catalog performs both functions at once. When the catalog is used literally, Traherne's technique is cumulative and extensive, largely derived from the extrovertive, positive way, and usually denotative of the "visible" external world, God's works, the smiling universe, and of divinity manifest in nature, including the human face and body. All the world is to be enjoyed. It is as if Traherne, by design and by the urgency of his joy, would present all the radiant world directly and immediately to us. When the catalog is used symbolically, his technique is appositive and intensive, and connotative of the "invisible" inner essential man, pneuma, or of the "invisible" Godhead or God. While each term in any one of Traherne's appositions may be broadly synonymous with the other terms, each also usually has a particular, distinctive meaning which it contributes to the development of the total idea. By such means as synonym, varied and incremental repetition, paradox, and symbol enriched by long tradition, Traherne would impart to us Self-knowledge and the dancing, laughing, loving Joy consequent upon it. He may be spoken of as making series of attempts, aiming series of shots at a target, in the hope that one or more series will for one or another reader hit the mark. In Traherne's poetry, the means of expression are suited to the mode of apprehension — what is the author's and what is to become the readers' mode of apprehension: direct, immediate, intuitive, open-eyed.

Three. Innocence: "The Salutation" to "The Preparative"

> *How like an Angel came I down!*
> "Wonder"

> *I must becom a Child again.*
> "Innocence"

THE DOBELL FOLIO BEGINS WITH relatively simple poems on original childhood; moves, generally speaking, through more complex poems in which childhood, original and redeemed, is by different modes described and in which there are more frequent and more fully developed references to the Fall; continues through poems which celebrate again the body and the created world and employ the redeemed intellect; and concludes with poems entitled "Thoughts" and highly ecstatic poems. This plan formally and stylistically reflects the spiritual progress of man from simple, innocent childhood through fallen, excessively conceptualized and verbalized experience to the years of the "philosophic mind" and redeemed, ecstatic Felicity. Understanding that any hard-and-fast dividing and categorizing of a unified sequence is apt to be somewhat artificial and arbitrary, we shall nevertheless find it critically accurate and useful to regard the Folio's threefold spiritual progress of Innocence, Fall, Redemption as corresponding to and being expressed by the groups of poems from (1) "The Salutation" to "The Preparative," (2) "The Instruction" to "Speed," (3) "The Designe" to "Goodnesse." [1] It is primarily by means of this pattern, Traherne's theme of childhood or the Christian myth of Regeneration, that Traherne "trace[s] the glorious Way Wherby thou may'st thy Highest Bliss enjoy" (p. 2).

There is not, however, a simple progression in the Folio. The progression has three distinct yet related complications. First, the nature and complexity of Traherne's subject necessitates a certain amount of doubling back, of incremental thematic repetition; for the sake of clarity, cogency, and the reader's fuller comprehension, the essential content requires repeated, varied expression. Secondly, as noted in the Introduction, the Dobell Folio has a twofold perspective, a double voice which both directs the way and keeps the goal immediately before us. When he is

writing spiritual autobiography of his past or writing *for* fallen
man, Traherne's assumed voice is often that of a man who has
not yet attained to Felicity. But Traherne also speaks from the
perspective of achieved mystic experience, in an "achieved" voice,
to men whom he hopes to bring to that Felicity which he enjoys.
This double voice helps to account for some of the shifts in
tense, of the recapitulatory passages, and of the frequent outbursts of ecstatic poetry reflecting Traherne's own Felicitous state
of being. However deliberately and consciously Traherne may
have used them, the shifts in tense and the ecstatic outbursts are
a grammatic and poetic way of implying that even when we are
most deeply fallen we are nevertheless in some sense always
united to God, who is nearer to us than we are to ourselves; in
St. Augustine's famous words, "Thou wert within, and I abroad
. . . Thou wert with me, but I was not with Thee." [2] The third
complication is that the Dobell Folio pervasively places greater
emphasis, even in the second group of poems, on the positive
aspects of experience, on the meaning of original and redeemed
childhood. A reason for this greater emphasis is apparently that,
as in *Christian Ethicks,* Traherne deliberately chose the strategy
of the positive approach as being the more effective one. In any
case, even though the second group of poems in D contains fuller
and more frequent references to fallen experience than the rest
of the Folio, the F poems (like the *Third Century*) are more
chronological, more overtly and simply sequential compared to
the richer, more complex unity of D.[3] This fact, especially, may
help to explain why so many critics, including even Margoliouth,
have for so long failed to see the Dobell Folio as a unified sequence, even though some of these same critics have commented
upon the grouping and order of the poems in F.

In accord with and in partial fulfillment of the Folio plan, the first three relatively simple poems, "The Salutation," "Wonder," and "Eden," use language almost entirely literally, including some of the key recurrent words. "The Salutation," linked to and immediately keeping the promise of "The Author to the Critical Peruser," celebrates the body and its birth into an earthly Eden. With such an aim and setting and written wholly in the present tense, the poem appropriately makes no explicit mention of sin at all. But Traherne is conscious craftsman enough to suggest the Fall and the fallen ego in the first stanza with the question, "Where was? in what Abyss, my Speaking Tongue?" For language is the ego's "other self," and we are later to read in the italicized, zeugmatic line from "Dumnesse," *"I then my Bliss did, when my Silence, break"* (p. 40). Because language "defines," conventionalizes, and standardizes vision, acquring language is tantamount to eating the apple, acquiring knowledge of good and evil. *Sub specie aeternitatis,* nothing is good or bad but thinking makes it so, and conceptualizing is only possible in and through language.

In his version of "The Salutation," Philip deleted stanza 6, which contains two of Thomas' most characteristic and vital ideas: the world is an "Eden so Divine and fair"; and man is God's "Son and Heir" (p. 6). This sixth stanza is the only one in the poem that is clearly and unambiguously pneuma-revealing. Thus Philip, by deleting it, immediately begins to defeat his brother's central purpose, begins to distort and disrupt the childhood theme, as well as to minimize the doctrine of the Golden Mean. This, in various ways, is Philip's typical and frequent practice, deleting or weakening many such passages. Judging by the changes he made, we shall learn that Philip was not only a bad versifier but also quite definitely no mystic. He apparently had no sympathy for or genuine understanding of many of his brother's mystical ideas. Might one reason why Thomas' poems were never published by his brother be that Philip finally decided it was impossible to remove or modify sufficiently all the "offensive" traces of Thomas' mysticism?

There is a double salutation in the poem: the speaker salutes the body, which in turn is saluted by God's works.

> These Brighter Regions which salute mine Eys
>   A Gift from God I take.
> The Earth, the Seas, the Light, the Day, the Skies,
> The Sun and Stars are mine; if those I prize.   (p. 6)

One notes that the catalog, including some basic "symbol words," is literal: Eyes, Light, Day, Sun. "Wonder" and "Eden," both poems opening very finely and continuing to sing the Self and "The Glorious Wonders of the Deitie" (p. 14), also repeatedly use the cumulative catalog. Philip characteristically shortens some of the catalogs (for example, "Wonder," line 61, and "Eden," line 15) by introducing a trite or stock adjective; thus he blunts their direct pointing. "Eden" demonstrates, as do other poems and prose passages, that Traherne associated the innocent child with unfallen Adam, that he understood the Garden myth of Genesis in a symbolic as well as literal, historic way, understood that Adam is indeed everyman and that the story of his original innocence, fall, and redemption in Christ, the Second Adam, is our own spiritual history and progress. And thus the Dobell Folio begins to appropriate, incorporate, pattern itself upon, the great Garden myth with its promise of redemption (Gen. 3:15) and the New Testament myth of Christ's fulfilling that promise.

Echoing the title "Wonder" and the word Wonders in the last line of "Eden," "Innocence" continues the analogy between Adam and the child, making it still more overt:

But that which most I Wonder at, which most
I did esteem my Bliss, which most I Boast,
And ever shall Enjoy, is that within
    I felt no Stain, nor Spot of Sin.

    . . . I was an Adam there,
    A little Adam in a Sphere
    Of Joys!   (pp. 14, 18)

The child, exactly like the unfallen Adam, apparently was without actual sin. Sin arises with conceptualizing, speaking, breaking
the silence in which the still Word is uttered by God and heard
by the inner Ear. Having suggested man's Fall indirectly and
negatively in the first four poems, Traherne announces in the
last line of "Innocence" with an assured and arresting suddenness
his central paradoxical theme: "I must becom a Child again"
(p. 18).

In contrast to the first three poems, which are mainly literal,
"Innocence," with its several paradoxes and more elaborate
triple-quatrain stanzaic form moving the poem toward greater
complexity, begins to use certain of the basic words in their
symbolic capacity. The subtlety, richness, and variety of Traherne's use of these words cannot of course be wholly indicated in
just one illustration, but the literal and symbolic use of "Light"
should be apparent by our contrasting a cumulative catalog
from "Eden" with several lines from "Innocence":

    Joy, Pleasure, Beauty, Kindness, Glory, Lov,
        Sleep, Day, Life, Light,
      Peace, Melody, my Sight,
    My Ears and Heart did fill, and freely mov.
                    ("Eden," p. 12)

What ere it is, it is a Light
  So Endless unto me
That I a World of true Delight
Did then and to this Day do see.

("Innocence," p. 18)

All poets, of course, use a word literally in one poem and the same word symbolically in another poem. But I know of no other poet who uses so many central words both literally and symbolically so consistently and repeatedly, or more purposefully. It should also be observed that in the last line of "Innocence" and the four lines just quoted from the same poem we have the appearance of the two voices which will become still more clear and distinct in subsequent poems: an assumed voice and a voice of an achieved and present possession of Delight or Felicity.

"The Preparative" uses symbolically words used literally in the previous poems and also introduces major symbols not at all employed earlier. For example, Eyes appears in an essentially literal way in the first three poems, and "Innocence" begins to imply the distinction between the conventional, unseeing eye and the third or truly seeing Eye; Sphere occurs only in "Innocence"; and the Mirror, Fountain, and Dwelling Place groups are seemingly unrepresented in the first four poems. On the other hand, six of the seven major classes appear in "The Preparative." Having expressed original childhood through one (appropriately literal) poetic means, Traherne turns, after his statement of theme at the end of "Innocence," to another mode (appropriately symbolic) in most of the subsequent poems in order to describe childhood, original and redeemed. Because of the profound, resonant symbolism of "The Preparative," key words become "colored," vibrate sympathetically, tend more so to be symbolic in the following poems, though these same words continue at times to be literal.

It is curious that critics have acclaimed the first four essentially literal and frequently anthologized poems as among Traherne's finest, if not actually the finest, and yet also have complained of his "prosiness" and have fancied that "he trusted reason too much, and imagination too little."[4] These facts imply that Traherne's particular literal use of language may be one quite effective quality of his poetry; that the charge of prosiness has to be re-examined; that perhaps criticism has not yet adequately, penetratingly, read and appreciated Traherne's more difficult and symbolic poems — to mention a few of the possible implications.

In order to explore some of these implications further as well as to illustrate in detail the gross nature and extent of Philip's disastrous revisions and to demonstrate that Traherne's literal catalogs and symbolic appositions are inherent to or grow out of his mystical subject matter, we should now closely examine "The Preparative," the first of the difficult, symbolic poems of the Dobell Folio and a poem which is central to an understanding of Traherne's work. Such an examination will show at length the working of Traherne's poetic in a single poem, will help to reveal his considerable craftsmanship, and will underscore the necessity of knowing some of the context of Traherne's meaning in order more fully and precisely to discover that meaning. Although we shall subsequently examine in some detail other poems, such as "Dumnesse," "My Spirit," the "Thoughts" poems, "Love," "Desire," and "Goodnesse," the following discussion of "The Preparative" is also intended to suggest the kind of thoroughgoing readings that Traherne's symbolic poems deserve and require if we are to evaluate them justly.

After the last line of "Innocence" states Traherne's central theme for fallen man, "I must becom a Child again," the next poem, "The Preparative," describes that pure vision, or mode of awareness, which must be recovered if fallen man is to be restored to his lost Felicity. The word preparative means preliminary, preparation, but the secondary and now obsolete medical meaning is also relevant: "something to prepare the system for medicine, or for a course of treatment."[5] As the word was often used figuratively, it might well refer to a preliminary step in the purgative stage of the *via mystica,* a step in the "course of treatment" for restoring the soul to "health." The preparation or preliminary step, as the last lines of the poem make clear, is retirement, a theme very familiar in Vaughan, or flight ("Flight is but the Preparative," "The Vision" tells us) from the contaminating, poisonous world of "Custom, Action, or Desire" ("The Instruction") in order to re-attain ultimately to wholesome, childlike innocence and vision. "The Preparative," as all else in Traherne, is founded upon the paradox central to Christianity and the contemplative tradition: "Except ye be converted, and become as little children, ye shall not enter into the kingdom of heaven" (Matt. 18:3).

Traherne's writing, like the language of all mysticism, is characteristically paradoxical, for the mystic consciousness is dialectical rather than logical or dualistic. Denying, as it were, logic, and frustrating logicians, professional and temperamental, paradox is a mode of expressing the miraculous. Traherne's world is one of "Glory, Love, Light, Space, Joy, Beauty and Varietie" ("The Vision," p. 26) — all of those shining words which exhilarate us; that is to say, it is, above all, a world of miracle. The miracle is the point where aspiration and reality meet, where things as we would have them, if only we knew our real desire and true interest, and things as they are, coincide. This coincidence obtains when our vision is clear and pure — "Evry Man naturaly seeing"

(*C* III 5). In *The Marriage of Heaven and Hell* Blake puts it succinctly: "If the doors of perception were cleansed, everything would appear to man as it is, infinite." We need, therefore, to regain the vision, the estate, the "Meditating Inward Ey," of the infant. Since the language of logic and common sense cannot adequately reveal the finite world as it is — infinite, miraculous — Traherne uses the language of paradox throughout "The Preparative" to describe that infant eye.

> My Body being Dead, my Lims unknown;
>> Before I skild to prize
>> Those living Stars mine Eys,
> Before my Tongue or Cheeks were to me shewn,
>> Before I knew my Hands were mine,   5
> Or that my Sinews did my Members joyn,
>> When neither Nostril, Foot, nor Ear,
> As yet was seen, or felt, or did appear;
>> I was within
> A House I knew not, newly clothd with Skin.   10
>
> (p. 20)

We must first note that both psychological investigations and our everyday notions affirm that the newborn infant, with whom the poem is centrally concerned, is in a state of extraordinary and highly limited sensory and intellectual apprehension; indeed, he is devoid of adult consciousness, without intellection, sensation, or activity in the ordinary sense. His sensations and activities are only automatic, spontaneous, uncontrolled, such as breathing, feeling heat, cold, and wetness, or making random bodily movements. The infant is, in fact, "mindless," and he does not distinguish between one and another external object.[6]

Nothing in the poem contradicts these facts or theories, and much supports them, even though the poem's essential meaning far transcends them. Most clearly, the first stanza emphasizes the infant's "mindlessness," or lack of self-consciousness, his fundamental lack of ideational knowledge. He does not know his body is his: "I was within A House I knew not." His limbs are "unknown"; he does not know how ("skild") to prize "Those living Stars mine Eys"; he does not know his hands are his or that his sinews join his members. Line 4 is a further development of the infant's lack of ordinary awareness and suggests his very restricted bodily activity. Lines 7–8 indicate that the infant is probably no more than a few weeks old, for he is unable to move his foot to a position where it will appear and be seen; he cannot purposefully move his hand in order to touch, feel, his nostril, foot, or ear. Nor, of course, can he see his nostril, foot or ear. The infant may, however, see above and about him objects other than his body; and his being, as developed in stanza 2, is concentrated in his extraordinary kind of sight:

> Then was my Soul my only All to me,
>> A Living Endless Ey,
>> Far wider then the Skie
> Whose Power, whose Act, whose Essence was to see.
>> I was an Inward *Sphere of Light,*   15
> Or an Interminable Orb of *Sight,*
>> An Endless and a Living Day,
> *A vital Sun* that round about did *ray*
>>> All Life and Sence,
> A Naked Simple Pure *Intelligence.*   20
>
>> (p. 20)

The state of being portrayed in the first two stanzas is comparable to the state of the soul prepared for the birth of Christ, as described by Eckhart: "the soul in which this birth is to happen must have purity and nobility of life, and be unitary and self-contained; it must not be dissipated in the multiplicity of things . . . In Being, however, there is no action and, therefore, there is none in the soul's essence . . . In that core of the soul is the central silence, the pure peace, and abode of the heavenly birth, the place for this event: this utterance of God's word." [7] The anonymous author of *The Cloud of Unknowing* — a work which shows the influence of Dionysius on every page and, in one chapter, quotes him as saying "the most godlike knowledge of God is that which is known by unknowing" — writes that God "cannot be comprehended by our intellect or any man's — or any angel's for that matter." [8] God is unknowable to the power of the rational intellect. Oddly, because of his bodily inactivity, his nonintellectual mode of apprehension, and his lack of self-awareness, the infant has thus already arrived at that destination toward which the adult student in the school of devotion must strive: "you are to forget not only all other things than yourself (and their doings — and your own!) but to forget also yourself . . . when all other things and activities have been forgotten (even your own) there still remains between you and God the stark awareness of your own existence. And this awareness, too, must go, before you experience contemplation in its perfection." [9]

As described by the literal catalog of stanza 1 and the contrasting symbolic appositions of stanza 2, in the uncorrupted child there is, in both the usual and the quite literal senses, no self-consciousness, no self-awareness, no division between knower and knowing; being and seeing are one. Before the infant's body is purposefully active, before he even knows he has or is a body (that is, before his latent powers of intellect and discrimination develop), the infant is not split, not divided in his consciousness. He does not look and, in effect, say to himself "I am looking," as the self-conscious adult does, knowingly or unknowingly. He simply looks and sees. His eye is single and his body full of light. For the infant's treasure is "to be true, Sincere and Single in a Blessed View" ("Dumnesse," p. 42). Not only, then, is there no sense of "my body" but there is even no sense of "I." Having no past from which abstractly to construct an ego, a mental picture of self, and no anxieties about or designs for the future, the infant can simply and wholly be his essential self: "Then was my Soul my only All to me," "Soul" here meaning, as often in Traherne, pneuma. When neither memory nor desire bind the self to past or future, when consciousness is empty with respect to the past and aimless with respect to the future, the void is filled with an infinitely expanded present. In childhood, "All Time was Eternity, and a Perpetual Sabbath" (*C* III 2). The child is outside of time. On this point the investigations of psychoanalysts confirm the intuitions of poets: the child "feels the imposition of adult time by adults as an alien intrusion into his own time, which is essentially in some sense infinite." [10] The infant's or child's consciousness or "Spirit filleth the whole World" (*C* I 30). Thus the infant is "A Living Endless Ey Far wider then the Skie" — because his power, act, essence is to see (note the infant is "defined" by an infinitive, not a substantive: as activity, not as thing); because he sees and *is* his seeing, he thereby embraces, is identical with or indistinguishable from, the sky and everything under, above, and around it. "For the Soul will by that means be the Sphere of His Omnipresence, and the Temple of the God-head: It will become ETERNITY, as *Trismegistus* speaketh, or ONE SPIRIT with God, as the Apostle. And then it must needs be present with all things *in Heaven, and in the Earth, and in the Sea,* as GOD is: for all things will be in it" (*CE,* p. 228).

This state, described in stanzas 1 and 2, is the innocent, unfallen, divine state, the rapturous condition of "Sweet Infancy"

("The Rapture"), the state prior to the debilitating and vitiating effects of education, custom, and convention, all of which impose the ultimately false, illusory separation between the "self" and the "not-self," between one's self and the rest of the world (*C* II 81, III 7). The entire poem (especially stanzas 2 and 6) is concerned with the nature of the real Self or pneuma. The self and the not-self, subject and object, are not so much two coins as they are opposite surfaces of the same coin, the reality of which lies "in between." The real Self, as opposed to the ego, cannot, after all, be a separately, intellectually knowable object; for what, then, is it that does the knowing? The Self escapes itself into an infinite regress in its own attempt at definition. It can no more become its own object of knowledge than a thumb can catch hold of itself. It is the relation to the supposedly outside and delimited, bounded object; or subject and object are the connected, continuous extreme ends of the middle ground which is the reality. The light needs the eye in order to be seen, just as the eye needs the light in order to see. Subject ("power") and object need each other, for "all satisfactions, Joys and Praises are the happy off-spring of Powers and Objects well united. Both the one and the other would lie void and barren if they never met together" (*CE*, p. 72; see also p. 264). Traherne's position does not constitute a denial of external reality or of an observing self. It merely asserts, affirms the truth, that object and subject exist only as abstractions from the concrete experience of perception, which experience "includes" subject and object as the end limits of a single, integrated reality. In his nonintellectual mode of being, the infant does not abstract from experience and divide it into subject and object. He simply perceives, experiences; he *is* the perception, the experience.

Nor should Traherne be charged, as he has been, with solipsism or egotism or the tendency toward either or both. Perhaps the best

— quickest, most efficient, and cogent — way to dismiss the charge is simply to point out that while the solipsist (and no professional philosopher is a solipsist) holds that only his mind (ego) is real and that all else exists in his fabricating mind, Traherne is perfectly aware that not he, as ego, but the spirit of God in him, the divine spark or image, is responsible for the joyous re-creation of the finite world. Is not Traherne's poem another way of saying what the contemplative tradition has anciently held — that God, through His Son, constantly and eternally creates the world and that "I live; yet not I, but Christ liveth in me" (Gal. 2:20)?

In a sense, then, the eye is the light, for without the other each is incomplete, unrealized. The "Or" in line 16 is not disjunctive; the "*Sphere of Light*" and the "Orb of *Sight*" are identical, or are two ways of describing the same reality. "The eye by which I see God," reads one of Eckhart's most famous paradoxical sayings, "is the same as the eye by which God sees me. My eye and God's eye are one and the same — one in seeing, one in knowing, and one in loving." [11] In the words of Plotinus:

He who then sees himself, when he sees will see himself a simple being, will be united to himself as such, will feel himself become such. We ought not even to say that he will *see,* but he will *be* that which he sees, if indeed it is possible any longer to distinguish seer and seen, and not boldly to affirm that the two are one. In this state the seer does not see or distinguish or imagine two things; he becomes another, he ceases to be himself and to belong to himself. He belongs to Him and is one with Him, like two concentric circles . . . Therefore this vision is hard to describe. For how can one describe, as other than oneself, that which, when one saw it, seemed to be one with oneself? [12]

We have noted that Traherne's poetry is often most effective when two of his main poetic characteristics combine, when, as in stanza 2 of "The Preparative," there is a catalog of concentrated images. The symbols Eye, Sphere, Light, Sun, and so forth (some of them compounded, like "Orb of *Sight*," to achieve even more intense effects) help to create a brilliant description of the ineffable vision that Plotinus discusses, of the miraculous event unfolding, line by line, before our eyes. Stanza 2 fairly bursts with light. The wonder is that Traherne could have achieved and sustained such a catalog of appositive images. For these symbols of divinity, eternity or the Eternal Now, and regeneration are exactly appropriate to Traherne's, the Christian mystic's, purpose in this poem. In themselves they say that the real nature of the infant, his soul or essential self, is united with God, is divine, is not only prepared for the birth of Christ but has received in the core of the soul God's Word. The quickening brilliance of the Divine Light, which penetrates, suffuses, fills the prepared soul, transfigures it into "An Endless and a Living Day." Knowing that "sun" is a symbol of God, particularly of the Second Person, the bringer of light and life, we more clearly understand that the divine child, whether he be an infant or a man reborn, is "*A vital Sun* that round about did *ray* All Life and Sence." Again, in a symbolic and highly poetic manner, Traherne is saying of the infant and of the redeemed man (for whom the infant is a metaphor), the man who has become again as a child, that he lives, yet not he but Christ in him. And Traherne's catalogs — or better, his appositive style, because this phrase includes not only nouns in apposition or juxtaposition but also verbs and adjectives in a series, and because it is free of derogatory associations — Traherne's appositive style is exactly appropriate for attempting to describe that indescribable vision, that union with the Godhead. For this

poetic manner seems to say, in effect, that what Traherne wishes
to describe is some tertium quid; paradoxically, it is this and
yet not this; it is this and yet that also. No wonder then that
Traherne's poetry is fundamentally and characteristically paradoxical. His appositive, paradoxical style is inherent to, or grows
out of, his mystical subject matter. Though often overlooked or
denied by previous criticism, there is indeed a vital and ineluicta-
ble connection between form and content, an organic oneness of
mode and meaning, in Traherne's poetry.

Philip's meddling with his brother's poetry may yet be turned
to some good: where we have both versions, a comparison can
be very instructive. Here is stanza 3 first in Thomas' and then in
Philip's version.

> I then no Thirst nor Hunger did conceiv,
>   No dull Necessity,
>   No Want was Known to me;
> Without Disturbance then I did receiv
>   The fair Ideas of all Things,   25
> And had the Hony even without the Stings.
>   A Meditating Inward Ey
> Gazing at Quiet did within me lie,
>   And evry Thing
> Delighted me that was their Heavnly King.   30
>   (p. 20)

> I then no Thirst nor Hunger did perceiv;
>   No dire Necessity
>   Nor Want was known to me:
> Without disturbance then I did receiv
>   The tru Ideas of all Things,   25
> The Hony did enjoy without the Stings.
>   A meditating inward Ey

Gazing at Quiet did within me ly,
　　And all things fair
Delighted me that was to be their Heir. 30
　　　　　　　　　　　　　　　　　(p. 21)

Philip's line 21, for example, is wrong and Thomas' is right.[13] Though the poem performs essentially at a higher level of meaning, I do not think it necessary to construe the poem in such a way as to be untrue to the fundamental facts of infancy. Of course the infant senses or feels or perceives hunger and thirst; no doubt, he gives himself wholly to it. Indeed, when an infant is hungry or thirsty, by Traherne's account, he *is* the hunger or thirst: "The Sence it self was I" ("My Spirit," p. 50). Lines 21–26, in Thomas' version, mean that the infant had no thoughts about, no conception of thirst, hunger, necessity, want. (Philip's change to "dire" in line 22 not only results in a cliché but, by suggesting a distinction between necessities that are dire and those that are not, also loses Thomas' implication that all necessity is dull, that anything less than the sense of absolute freedom is intolerable, this sense of freedom being correlative with Traherne's sense of joy and consequent upon perfect obedience to God's Will.) *Knowing* no necessity or want, the infant is comparable to the birds and lilies of the Gospel, which take no thought for the morrow, no thought for what they shall eat or what they shall drink. Without disturbing anxieties, being "mindless" or with "A Mind thats unpossest," without bodily or mental activities of the usual kind, the infant purely receives the fair ideas, the impressions of all things as they *really* are. He lives in eternity, for, as Kierkegaard says, "time does not really exist without unrest; it does not exist for dumb animals who are absolutely without anxiety." [14]

Although certain important differences between Traherne and Platonic philosophy are apparent — as, for example, Traherne's enthusiastic praise in contrast to Plato's depreciation, relatively speaking, of the physical world and of sense perception — one is inclined to assent to Margoliouth's annotation of "Ideas" in line 25: "Pure Platonism." But because, as Whitehead suggested, the history of Western philosophy is a series of footnotes to Plato, because Plato's poetic-philosophic writings permit a variety of interpretations, we must briefly indicate the kind of Platonism that stanza 3 is not and the kind that it is.

Plato distinguishes between several types of knowledge, among which are "opinions," which include all sense-derived knowledge, and rational insight, the objects of which are Ideas, the Platonic Forms or Archetypes, arrived at, according to some interpreters, by the discursive, conceptualizing intellect. In this view, sense knowledge is not true knowledge; conceptual knowledge, since it is conversant with the universal, immutable, and essential Ideas, is consequently the only genuine knowledge. The Ideas are said to be apprehended by the mature philosopher's discursive reason, not by the senses or intuition. This kind of rationalistic Platonism does not obtain in stanza 3 nor elsewhere in Traherne.

On the other hand, it may be argued from *The Symposium* and *The Republic,* for example, that Plato describes a progression of vision which moves from sense perception, to moral and intellectual understanding, to direct intuitive apprehension. The final vision of which Diotima speaks in *The Symposium* is a religious rather than an intellectual experience and cannot be adequately communicated by ordinary verbal means. Similarly, in *The Republic,* when Glaucon asks for an account of the Good, Socrates, the master of definition, confesses that such an account is beyond his powers. He then employs poetic devices, the analogy of the sun with the Good and the allegory of the cave, in order to give his audience some notion of the Good. (This whole procedure is of course characteristically mystical.) In the discussion of the "four stages of cognition," which precedes the allegory of the cave, Socrates distinguishes between the state of mind (*dianoia*) which grasps mathematical objects and the state of mind (*noesis*) which grasps the supreme Form of the Good. As F. M. Cornford explains, "*dianoia* suggests discursive thinking or reasoning from premiss to conclusion, whereas *noesis* is constantly compared to the immediate act of vision and suggests rather the direct intuition or apprehension of its object." [15] It is this mystical and, I believe, critically central part of Plato's thinking which Traherne appears to have responded to and emphasized most, as other Neoplatonists did.

Plotinus, for example, remarks that "the discursive reason, if it wishes to say anything, must seize first one element of the Truth and then another; such are the conditions of discursive thought. But how can discursive thought apprehend the absolutely simple? . . . in the vision that which sees is not reason, but something presupposed by reason, as is the object of vision." [16] The discursive reason moves step by step, from point to point. But the infant eye is one-pointed, in the sense of that divine Sphere whose central point is everywhere ("My Spirit," p. 50). Since the vision is an undivided unity, discursive reason cannot operate here. That which sees the vision, so to speak, is the intuitive faculty. "Intuition," in its seventeenth-century meaning, is "the immediate knowledge ascribed to angelic and spiritual beings, with whom vision and knowledge are identical" (OED). It is in this sense that Milton, for example, uses the term "Intuitive" in *Paradise Lost* (V, 488). Thomas' description of the infant is precisely right: "My Body being Dead . . . Then was my Soul my only All to me . . . A Naked Simple Pure *Intelligence*," and (from "Wonder") "How like an Angel came I down!" [17] Again, "conceiv" is the exact word. Traherne chooses his words with the precision expected of a poet, and Philip's "correcting," here falsifying and sentimentalizing the meaning of childhood, would reduce the poem to confusion. The infant's mode of apprehension is intuitive; he does not conceptualize. Because he has no cumbersome, interfering conception of his body, of thirst, hunger, necessity, want, and so on, he immediately, purely receives "The fair Ideas of all Things And [has] the Hony even without the Stings."

Philip, perhaps thinking of the rationalistic kind of Platonism and almost certainly thinking of conceptual knowledge and hence of truth and falsity, mistakenly changes Thomas' adjective "fair" in line 25 to "tru." Thomas is talking about the fairness or beauty of all sense data and intuitive data as the infant purely sees them without customary distinctions, unspoiled by the assigning of conventional values. Lines 27–30, which epitomize the first three stanzas and make overt the crucial idea of the infant's delight and heavenly kingship, support the view that the infant enjoys both of the two historic kinds of mystical experience: the extraordinary sensory experience as well as the deeper intuitive vision. (The first is that of the infant's looking outward through his eyes and seeing the Divine Light shining through the transfigured physical world; the second is his looking inward and finding the Divine Being at the depths of his soul.) To the counsel to seek first the kingdom of God (Matt. 6:33) must be added the wisdom that "the kingdom of God is within you" (Luke 17:21). Having no past and taking no thought for the morrow, the inner infant eye, the Third Eye, "Gazing at Quiet," whether it be looking outward or inward, is concentrated wholly upon and within the Eternal Now. "Gazing at Quiet" is an essential precondition to attaining the beatific vision, for "it is in the stillness, in the silence, that the word of God is to be heard. There is no better avenue of approach to this Word than through stillness, through silence." [18] "Wise Nature," we read in "Dumnesse," made the infant "Deaf" so "that he might Not be disturbd" by language in its discursive, dualis-

tic character, "Nor Injurd by the Errors and the Wrongs That
Mortal Words convey" (p. 40).

At the end of stanza 3, Philip made additional changes. Although "Heir" of his line 30 is not inappropriate with respect to
"inherits" in line 31, the timidity of line 30 and the nonsense of
"was to be," written no doubt for the sake of meter, are characteristic and revealing "corrections." Philip's line 30 loses contact
especially with such lines as 12–13 and 18–19 (but see, also, what
Philip has done to those lines). And his "was to be," implying fu-
turity, simply contradicts Thomas' view that the infant as infant
is the true inheritor and the king of all the world, and later,
largely through custom and bad education, "was to be" not the
heir or king but the fallen man — hence the necessity of becoming like unto a child or infant again. Apart from its especial con-
sistency with certain preceding lines, Thomas' "Heavnly King"
is right and effective because the infant, realizing his essential
divinity, is, paradoxically, the creator of the fair ideas of all things
he purely receives. The *simple* act of perception is a divine act of
creation. "Is it not written in your law, I said, Ye are gods?"
(John 10:34; see Ps. 82:6).

Philip changed "And evry Thing" to "And all things fair."
Christian Ethicks reads: "Humility regards *all Objects, high and
low, Good and Evil:* but with a peculiar remark and notice of its
own. It takes them in another light, and discerns them all with
another kind of sence. It is in some manner the taste of the Soul"
(p. 208, italics supplied; the whole chapter on humility makes it
clear that to acquire humility is to become like unto a child).
The *Centuries* read: "*All Things* were made to be yours . . . The
End for which you were Created is that by Prizing *all* that God
hath don, you may Enjoy your self and Him in Blessedness" (I,
12, italics supplied). If only Philip's version of Thomas' poems
existed, imagine the inconsistencies Thomas might be accused of.

It seems clear from his line that Philip, concerned with conceptual knowledge and unappreciative of the significance of Thomas' lines, would make vitiating distinctions between God's works: some are fair, some not. On the other hand, Thomas says unequivocally, without any qualification or reservation, that everything delighted the infant. The infant has no conceptual knowledge and no convention which would distinguish this as fair, that as foul, but "in another light" sees *all* purely. As the famous passages from the beginning of *The Third Century* read: "All appeared New, and Strange at the first, inexpressibly rare, and Delightfull, and Beautifull . . . All Things were Spotles and Pure and Glorious: yea, and infinitly mine, and Joyfull and Precious" (III, 2). All delights the infant, the "Heavenly King," the "Naked Simple Pure *Intelligence*." It is a matter of simple seeing, of right apprehension. Or, as St. Augustine tells us, "to the healthy and pure internal eye He is everywhere present." [19] Now the adult sees darkly through the glass of mind and custom; then, as child, he saw and, reborn, will see in the clear light of the healthy, inner eye.

Partly through a catalog of the senses, the themes of delight and heavenly kingship are developed and further explained in stanza 4:

> For *Sight* inherits Beauty, *Hearing* Sounds,
>   The *Nostril* Sweet Perfumes,
>   All *Tastes* have hidden Rooms
> Within the *Tongue;* and *Feeling Feeling* Wounds
>   With Pleasure and Delight: but I   35
> Forgot the rest, and was all Sight, or Ey.
>   Unbodied and Devoid of Care,
> Just as in Heavn the Holy Angels are.
>   For Simple Sence
> Is Lord of all Created Excellence.   (p. 22)   40

We may wonder why the infant seems to feel no pain.[20] No doubt, infancy has its full share of pain, and Traherne does not adopt the naive position that the infant is without pain. Rather, Traherne knows that the unfallen infant *is* the pain, *is* the hunger or thirst; in short, he knows that the egoless experience is always literally ecstatic. Yet it is to Traherne's purpose to emphasize delight and pleasure because God's law commands the enjoyment of all his works, and the right valuing of the world leads straight to enjoying it (*C* I 12). By the very right of his senses (*C* I 21) and with the right ("extraordinary") use of his senses the infant, or the man reborn, enjoys the world and accomplishes God's purpose. All things are to be enjoyed. "Even Trades them selvs seen in Celestial Light, And Cares and Sins and Woes are Bright" ("The Vision," p. 26). "Seen in Celestial Light," even pain is "Bright." Ultimately, Traherne is talking about a state beyond pleasure and pain, a state including yet transcending joy and suffering: the state of blessedness or, in Traherne's word, Felicity. "Happiness [that is, blessedness] is God," Eckhart writes,

and all those who are happy are, in the act of happiness, God and the divine nature and substance of God. St. Paul says: 'He who being naught, thinketh himself aught, deceiveth himself.' In the act of happiness he is brought to naught and no creaturehood exists for him. As the worthy Dionysius says: 'Lord, lead me to where thou art a nothingness,' meaning: lead me, Lord, to where thou transcendest every created intellect: for as St. Paul declares: 'God dwells in a light that no man can approach unto'; that is: God is not to be discerned in any created light whatever . . . As David says: 'Lord in thy light' ["Celestial Light"] shall we see light': with the divine nature we shall conceive the perfection of the divine nature, which alone is our entire felicity, here in grace and there in perfect happiness.[21]

Achieving this felicity, Eckhart says elsewhere, "must be done by means of forgetting and losing self-consciousness . . . a man should diminish his senses and introvert his faculties until he achieves forgetfulness of things and self."[22] Being un-self-conscious, forgetting his other senses and concentrating his being in "Sight, or Ey," the infant naturally is in that state which the author of *The Cloud of Unknowing* advises the adult contemplative to strive for: "if ever you are to come to this cloud and live and work in it, as I suggest, then just as the cloud of unknowing is as it were above you, between you and God, so you must also put a cloud of forgetting beneath you and all creation"; for "in perfect contemplation . . . everything less than God is completely forgotten, as it ought to be."[23] God is to be discerned neither in the light of the "created intellect" nor in the light of "created" or ordinary sense perception; the self is to be brought to naught, to have no consciousness of itself. An analogy in *Christian Ethicks* is elucidating: "The Eye is far more sensible of the Day, and of the beauty of the Universe, than it is of it self, and is more affected with that light it beholds, than with its own essence. Even so the Soul when it sees GOD is sensible only of the glory of that eternal Object: All it sees is GOD, it is unmindful of it self. It infinitely feels him, but forgets it self in the Rapture of its Pleasure" (p. 264).

"Unbodied and Devoid of Care" — unconscious of his body and without the anxieties which ego is heir to — the infant, with the image of God in him undulled, has no need, as the fallen adult has, "to Grow up into Him," because the infant is already "filled with the Fulness of his Godhead," whose "Essence also is the Sight of Things" (*C* II 84). "For Simple Sence is Lord of all

Created Excellence." The child's or reborn man's simple act of perception re-creates the otherwise dead material world and praises and delights God in so accomplishing his purpose. God's world is so constructed that the eye and the object are completed and fulfilled in each other in the pure, delightful, and apocalyptic act of re-creation. In that act, the divine, pneuma-inspired universe destroys, transforms, replaces the dead world of psyche, custom, and selfish solicitude. The proper use of the senses is enjoyment: re-creation is recreation. The natural world is the Spirit of God at play.

The fifth stanza more overtly confirms what the first four stanzas and the first four poems have suggested and implied: the infant is born without actual sin.

> Be'ing thus prepard for all Felicity,
>   Not prepossest with Dross,
>   Nor stifly glued to gross
> And dull Materials that might ruine me,
>   Not fetterd by an Iron Fate   45
> With vain Affections in my Earthy State
>   To any thing that might Seduce
> My Sence, or misemploy it from its use
>   I was as free
> As if there were nor Sin, nor Miserie.   50
>   (p. 22)

As the first line indicates, the preceding stanzas have described the soul "prepard for all Felicity"; subsequent lines of this stanza develop what that soul was not. It was not "prepossest" by or rigidly attached to any thing which would "ruine" it — that is, in the etymological sense, cause its Fall; and it was not bound by "an Iron Fate." Hence Traherne can conclude the stanza, "I was as free As if there were nor Sin, nor Miserie." The question of Traherne's view of original sin is problematic; yet not only stanza 5 but also other passages in his writing suggest that he denies certain "unorthodox" and "ultraorthodox" doctrines of Original Sin (that is, Pelagian, Jansenist, Calvinist, and some Lutheran doctrines), and that he adopts a position which affirms the infant's total innocence, with the qualification that he admits, in accord with Anglican doctrine, that a tendency or inclination to evil exists in man.[24]

It is indisputably clear that Traherne is not among those who pushed the teaching of St. Augustine so far as to assert the total corruption of human nature. On the other hand, some critics have mistakenly regarded Traherne as a Pelagian. Traherne writes "that our Misery proceedeth ten thousand times more from the outward Bondage of Opinion and Custom, then from any inward corruption or Depravation of Nature: And that it is not our Parents Loyns, so much as our Parents lives, that Enthrals and Blinds us," but he immediately adds, "Yet is all our Corruption Derived from Adam: inasmuch as all the Evil Examples and inclinations of the World arise from His Sin" (*C* III 8). Pelagius denied any corruption of human nature and held that Adam's sin injured no one but himself. He attributed the widespread existence of sin to the following of Adam's example; the existence of original sin, so far as he allowed that it existed at all, was due to purely external causes. On the contrary, although Traherne speaks in degrees and ascribes greater importance to "outward Bondage," he does not deny "inward corruption" but affirms that it derives from Adam, and to "Examples" he adds the very crucial "inclinations." And in *Christian Ethicks,* he lists among "natural doctrines" the doctrine that "man is a Sinner, that he is prone to Evil" (p. 118). That is, Traherne's position, rather than being Pelagian, is much closer to the Anglican doctrine of Original Sin, which is interpreted to mean that human nature is corrupt insofar as it possesses a tendency ("inclinations") to evil. To speak of a proneness or tendency toward or potentiality for evil is necessarily to imply an opposite tendency toward or potentiality for good. Traherne's outlook and his characteristic choice of strategy naturally emphasize this inclination toward good; for this emphasis, while not contradictory to Anglican doctrine, is exactly in accord with Traherne's own experience, and his radical empiricism and thoroughgoing honesty require the articulation of it. Furthermore, it may very well be that Traherne was more concerned to rebut the contemporary, flourishing, and therefore more immediately dangerous doctrines of "total depravity" than to confute the remoter Pelagianism, which had been more than adequately countered by Augustine. That of course does not make of Traherne a Pelagian.

Traherne, then, particularly rejects those heterodox versions of the doctrine of Original Sin which by asserting or overemphasizing man's depravity deny, in effect, free will. Freedom occupies a central place in Traherne's thinking, as it does in Milton's. Man has the freedom to choose, and just as all his corruption derives from the First Adam so man can choose wisely through the aid and example of the Second Adam. To the extent that one insists upon man's innate evil, one denies the Original and continued, though often obscured, Goodness of pneuma, denies man's meaningful participation in the free choice of moral good, and thereby also tends to render the Incarnation and Crucifixion meaningless. Without hinging the whole argument on capitalization or the lack of it (Traherne's capitalization practice is not that consistent), we may suggest that Traherne regards the unfallen child as premoral, neither good nor evil, but more inclined to transcendent Good and therefore also to moral good; "I was ten thousand times more prone to Good and Excellent Things, then evil" (*C* III 8). Traherne begins the *Centuries* with this simile: "An Empty Book is like an Infants Soul, in which any Thing may be Written" (*C* I 1). The *Third Century,* "The Preparative," and much else attest that we may legitimately reverse the terms of the simile in order to indicate accurately Traherne's view of the infant: an infant's soul is like an empty book, all potentiality. The infant is wholly without actual lowercase good or evil, and this is consistent with Anglican doctrine. "But I was quickly tainted and fell by others" (*C* III 8). The child learns moral good and evil; he eats the apple of the tree of the knowledge of good and evil. He falls from innocent emptiness "by the Customs and maners of Men . . . by the Impetuous Torrent of Wrong Desires in all others whom I saw or knew . . . finaly by the Evil Influence of a Bad Education" (*C* III 7); and thus the wrong though weaker potential or tendency is realized. One advantage, then, that the saint enjoys over the child is that he knows not only transcendent Good, as the unfallen child does, but also the moral good which he freely chooses.

It is no surprise that stanza 5 seems to deny materialism as well as "unorthodox" and "ultraorthodox" doctrines of Original Sin, for, perhaps in part because of Manichaean influences, materialism and a belief in man's innate evil often go hand in hand. Like other passages in Traherne, stanza 5 is suggestive of Berkeley. The view that the objects of our senses are sensible and not material does not deny or wish away the world but asserts firmly the reality of the sensible world. What is denied is not matter as "objects of sense" but the abstract "matter" of materialism, matter understood as gross, inert, material stuff, an invisible, intangible substrate which cannot be seen or touched or otherwise sensed. (This concept of matter has indeed been disposed of by modern science.) Such was the position of Berkeley, who believed materialism to be the root of dualism, skepticism, atheism. Such was, I think, even before Berkeley, the position of Traherne. Just as

Berkeley saw the necessity of refuting Locke's materialism, so Traherne perhaps saw the necessity of answering Hobbes' materialism and skeptical view of man as inherently evil and selfish.[25] For if one believes that ultimate reality consists of an unperceivable material substrate, if one thinks of the world as material things, he may be further deceived by "vain Affections" into thinking he selfishly should or could grasp and possess the things of this world (*C* III 7–14). The laying waste of natural powers through a life of greedy getting and spending and the sense-seducing belief in separate, bounded material things are products of the ego and conceptualizing intellect. On the other hand, the egoless and nonintellectual infant or child, who does not *think* of himself and the world as body or material thing, blissfully regards the flower for what he can see in it, not for what commercial and profitable perfume he can squeeze out of it. Having no "body" and no "mind" to fetter the spirit, he is not "stifly" attached to "dull Materials that might ruine" him but rather is free properly to use his senses in simple sensing, is precisely free of sin, that is, of taking the illusion, the thing, as an outside and separate reality. He is thus free of the consequence of sin, "Miserie," which is the negation of bliss or felicity.

> For not the Objects, but the Sence
> Of Things, doth Bliss to Souls dispence,
>   And make it Lord like Thee.   ("Desire," p. 179)

As an Eastern writer has phrased it: "only when you have nothing in your mind and no mind in things are you vacant and spiritual, empty and marvelous."[26]

Centuries before Traherne's day, the writings of Dionysius the pseudo-Areopagite became an intrinsic part of Christian knowledge, particularly among the medieval mystics. The enthusiasm of the Middle Ages for the pseudo-Areopagite was shared by Renaissance writers, including such figures familiar to Traherne as Ficino, who translated Dionysius, and Pico, who found in the pseudo-Areopagite a fellow esoteric thinker. Although Traherne of course could not have been directly influenced by the Eastern writer just quoted, he would have directly or indirectly known the *via negativa* of Dionysius: "Unto this Darkness which is beyond Light we pray that we may come, and may attain unto vision through the loss of sight and knowledge, and that in ceasing thus to see or know we may learn to know that which is beyond all perception and understanding (for this emptying of our faculties is true sight and knowledge)."[27] This emptiness which is, paradoxically, a fullness of effulgent beatitude is a universal theme of mysticism, East and West, and it appears clearly in stanza 6 of "The Preparative":

> Pure Empty Powers that did nothing loath,
>> Did like the fairest Glass,
>> Or Spotless polisht Brass,
> Themselvs soon in their Objects Image cloath.
>> Divine Impressions when they came,   55
> Did quickly enter and my Soul inflame.
>> Tis not the Object, but the Light
> That maketh Heaven; Tis a Purer Sight.
>> Felicitie
> Appears to none but them that purely see.   60
>
>   (p. 22)

Other poems and works of Traherne also develop the concept of the soul as an empty mirror which purely receives and is filled with *all* "Divine Impressions." "For as a Looking Glass is nothing in Comparison of the World, yet containeth all the World in it, and seems a real fountain of those Beams which flow from it so the Soul is Nothing in respect of God, yet all Eternity is contained in it, and it is the real fountain of that Lov that proceedeth from it" (*C* IV 84). Just as any container can be most fully filled when it is, to begin with, most completely empty, so he who completely humbles himself, who is entirely empty, egoless, will be exalted, completely filled with felicity. Humility, Traherne says in *Christian Ethicks,* "is like a Mirror lying on the ground with its face upwards: All the height above increaseth the depth of its Beauty within, nay, turneth it into a new depth . . . Humility is the fittest Glass of the Divine Greatness, and the fittest Womb for the conception of all Felicity" (p. 209).

The "humble" condition of the infant is precisely the most receptive one: minimal bodily state, nonintellectual mode of being, and simple — that is, not ordinary, conventional, conceptualizing — sensing concentrated in sight. "The eye and the soul," Eckhart affirms, "are also mirrors."[28] The infant's "Empty Powers" loath nothing because, like a mirror, they see, receive, all "Divine Impressions" purely. If, as Genesis tells us, all God's creation is good, then that is how all of it ought to be regarded, actually seen. Like an empty mirror and loathing nothing, the infant truly loves all. "If God dwelleth in the Soul as the Sun in a Mirror, while it looketh upon him, the love of God must needs issue from that Soul, for God *is love,* and his love is in it" (*CE,* p. 264).

We cannot leave stanza 6 without remarking specifically on a few additional points. First, by contrast with Thomas' line 51, Philip's "Pure nativ Powers that Corruption loath" not only suggests narrow moralism, little imagination, and misunderstanding or deliberate perversion of his brother's poetry but also implies misunderstanding of or quarrel with the contemplative tradition. Secondly, it is remarkable how well the poem has prepared us for stanza 6 and how this stanza reflects back upon the poem.

Thomas' "Pure Empty Powers that did nothing loath" is an apt and, one feels, inevitable sequence to the preceding stanzas; and even "Spotless polisht Brass" signals Traherne's artistry in the reflexive use of language, for the phrase echoes the implication of stanza 5 that the infant is without sin or "spot." Because the infant soul is free and empty (prepared), divine impressions "quickly enter" and inflame it; "quickly" of course is being played upon. And because the soul is so quickened, so enlightened, it is, as stanza 2 reads, a *"Sphere of Light,"* "An Endless and a Living Day," *"A vital Sun* that round about did *ray* All Life and Sence." Most of the words of stanza 2 and other words, such as preparative, conceive, honey, ruin, stifly, free, empty, and quickly, especially reveal Traherne's artistry, his exact and reflexive use of language. The language of the poem continually works reflexively upon itself, expanding and elucidating its meaning. Thirdly, "Subject" could be substituted for "Object" in "'Tis not the Object, but the Light That maketh Heaven; Tis a Purer Sight"; however, in his day Traherne had to contend not with subjectivism, in any of its various forms, but with materialism and the commonsensical faith in objects, things. That Traherne is himself not a subjectivist is apparent from his opposing against "Object" not "Subject" but "Light." "The Light . . . maketh Heaven; Tis a Purer Sight" implies that felicity is a matter of right apprehension, to which point the poem has led us all along. Moreover, "Light" imports "Spirit"; it is the Spirit of God that is at work in and at one with the pure infant soul. And whenever we mention "spirit" in connection with Traherne we should remind ourselves of Traherne's praise of and thanksgivings for the body and for all creation; we should recall how often Traherne must have leaped with rapture for being alive and in the flesh. If his spirit soared ecstatically among the heavens, his feet danced joyfully upon the earth. Traherne's mysticism is neither vague nor groundless.

The final stanza, in Traherne's intense appositive style, recapitulates the description, in the six preceding stanzas, of the infant soul or eye, and it drives home, to the fallen man, the theme of regeneration, of retiring from the entangled, bound world of psyche to the state of redeemed childhood, of freedom and felicity:

> A Disentangled and a Naked Sence
>   A Mind thats unpossest,
>   A Disengaged Brest,
> An Empty and a Quick Intelligence
>   Acquainted with the Golden Mean,   65
> An Even Spirit Pure and Serene,
>   Is that where Beauty, Excellence,
> And Pleasure keep their Court of Residence.
>   My Soul retire,
> Get free, and so thou shalt even all Admire.   70
>
> (p. 24)

This kind of piling up of attributes, all intended to present the object with greater effectiveness, is found also in Herbert and Vaughan, perhaps most famously in Herbert's "Prayer" and in the fifth and sixth stanzas of the Silurist's "The Night." Whether or not Traherne is stylistically indebted to Herbert and Vaughan, stanza 7 is, in any case, no mere, careless listing of phrases. Lines 61–66 not only summarize the ideas of the preceding stanzas (and even repeat key words) but also arrange the nouns in what is usually taken as an ascending order of value: Sence, Mind, Brest, Intelligence,[29] Spirit. That these lines, which at first appear only cumulative, are not merely in juxtaposition but in some kind of apposition is indicated by the related and synonymous adjectives, by the singular verb "Is," by "that," and by the state of the infant as described in the poem. "Remark the seeming identity of body and mind in infants," Coleridge enjoins,[30] to which we might add that the infant or redeemed man is a wholly integrated being, Sence, Mind, Brest, Intelligence, Spirit.

In *Christian Ethicks,* Traherne writes, "All Things by a kind of Temperance are made and ordered in Number, Weight and Measure, so that they give and receive a Beauty and Perfection" (*CE,* pp. 179–180). God, Traherne argues, could have made man and the world infinite in bulk, but the natural, finite world "pleaseth him infinitely Better, and so will it please us, when we are Wise as He is" (*CE,* p. 180), that is, when we are "Acquainted with the Golden Mean," when we see the ordered harmony of all things, the interrelatedness of all things by which each has its being and beauty. The infant is naturally so acquainted, and thus he receives "the fair Ideas of all Things" and everything delights him who is "their Heavnly King." "For the same Wisdom which created the World, is the only Light wherein it is enjoyed" (*CE,* p. 184). Traherne is here of course paraphrasing David: "Lord in thy light shall we see light." In "Celestial Light," "the Light That maketh Heaven," even a grain of sand is seen and enjoyed as perfect and infinite in profit, splendor, and delight.

> And thus a Sand is Endless, though most small.
> And every Thing is truly Infinite,
> In its Relation deep and exquisite.   (*CE,* p. 181)

If God's natural world is perfect, then so is the unfallen natural man; that is, the newborn infant is without actual sin. Even man's fall from innocence, due largely to the effect of corrupting custom and bad education on the tendency to evil, is ultimately fortunate (a subject to be discussed in the next chapter's account of the Fall group of poems). Thus follows the counsel of retirement to the fallen man, so that he will "even all Admire," see all as perfect, see the harmony, the relation of one element or aspect of the world to another. The miracle is that the world as we would have it, if only we knew our true interest and desire, is God's world as it is, if only we could see that world through an infant or redeemed eye. The phrase "Golden Mean" "gathers up" and is elucidated by the rest of the poem; it, as all else, is to be understood in the context of the poem, of the unified sequence of poems which the Dobell Folio is, of Traherne's other major writings, and of the contemplative tradition.

In line 68, "Court of Residence," there is a gathering symbol too, or at least one that harks back to the first stanza, "I was within a House I knew not," looks forward to line 5 of "The Vision," "the Godheads Dwelling Place," and then resounds throughout the Dobell Folio. Not knowing the House it was within, the infant soul dwelled in the temple or divine palace "where Beauty, Excellence, And Pleasure keep their Court of Residence." "Know ye not that ye are the temple of God, and that the Spirit of God dwelleth in you?" (I Cor. 3:16). "Lord, thou hast been our dwelling place in all generations" (Ps. 90:1). Medieval mystics, allegorists, and poets celebrated the womb of Mary, wherein Christ or pneuma lodges, in dwelling-place symbolism: "palace," "bower," and "garden enclosed." During the Renaissance, metaphors of the body-soul as a temple or castle, as in Spenser's *Faerie Queene,* Book II, carried an enriched, traditional force. The author of *The Temple,* perhaps the single major literary influence on Traherne, concludes "Man":

> Since then, my God, thou hast
> So brave a Palace built; O dwell in it,
> That it may dwell with thee at last!

And Traherne, who in the *Centuries* prays "that I may Dwell in Him, and He in me" (I, 97), concludes "The Preparative" by counseling fallen man to return Home, to become, as the child, free of sin and misery, to retire from the dark cave of custom, action, and desire into the illuminating natural and divine Light.

Four. Fall: "The Instruction" to "Speed"

> *My Heart did Hard remain*
> *Long time: I sent my God away,*
> *Grievd much that he could not impart his Joy.*
> "The Approach"

> *The Inward Work is the Supreme: for all*
> *The other were occasiond by the Fall.*
> "Silence"

SEVERAL OF THE FOLIO'S LEAST SYMBOLIC poems may well have been written earlier and "revised" and inserted in the Dobell sequence. "The Instruction," which begins the Fall group of poems, was in Margoliouth's opinion inserted at the last minute between the two connected poems, "The Preparative" and "The Vision" (II, 342); this hortatory poem contains only one major symbol, "Eys" (line 10). "The Approach," which according to Margoliouth is a "later version" of *C* III 4 (II, 346), has only the same major symbol (line 25). (And there may be some question whether "Eys" actually functions symbolically in these two poems.) "The Apprehension" contains no symbols; the seven lines of this fragment "are obviously all that Thomas thought worth keeping of a longer poem" (II, 351). "Blisse" consists of two "revised" stanzas from "The Apostacy" in F and is crossed out in manuscript, though not necessarily by Philip as Margoliouth remarks (II, 393); it has no major symbols, for the words crowns and eyes are used only in their literal sense. Excepting these four poems, which may all have been afterthought insertions, the Dobell Folio quite possibly was entirely or largely conceived and written as a whole some time after 1668.[1]

These four essentially nonsymbolic poems are mainly concerned with fallen or nonfelicitous states, three of them actually appearing in the middle, Fall group. (Most of the references in the Folio to the fallen state and to the need for purgation appear in lines or stanzas, rather than whole poems, within this middle group.) "The Approach" is the longest and best of the four; the wisdom of including the other three may be questioned, for they are the least successful poems in the Folio. Did Traherne, whose poetic abilities in the Dobell Folio are clearly better elicited and displayed on themes of innocence, felicity, and redemption than on the fallen state, feel, perhaps after submitting his manuscript to a friend's scrutiny and suggestions, that the Folio needed more poems on the Fall and purgation and so proceed to insert such poems from material he had on hand? "The Instruction" may have been inserted in order also to mark more clearly and distinctly the transition from the state of innocence (portrayed in "The Salutation" to "The Preparative") to the fallen state (variously described in "The Instruction" to "Speed"). That Traherne could write whole effective poems on the fallen state appears evident from such poems as "Solitude" (a fine poem in spite of Philip's probable tampering with it) and the very interesting "Thy Turtle Doves O Lord to Dragons turn" in the "Select Meditations."

We have seen that, having awakened us to the need for redemption, to the desire for union, as expressed in the last line of "Innocence," "I must becom a Child again," the speaker then describes in the highly symbolic terms of "The Preparative" the state of childhood or infancy, urging in the last two lines retirement or flight from the fallen world and self as a preparatory, purgative step on the path toward Felicity. The fallen adult is then instructed in the necessity of purgation and repentance:

> Spue out they filth, thy flesh abjure;
> Let not Contingents thee defile.
> For Transients only are impure,
> And Aery things alone beguil.   (p. 24)

This stanza, as indeed the rest of "The Instruction," is unusual in the Dobell sequence for its rather forceful and insistent hortatory tone. One feels the poem should be read loudly, very loudly, with perhaps even a clenched-fist desk-slamming at the end. It is not that the phrase "thy flesh abjure" is contrary to Traherne's various celebrations of and thanksgivings for the body and the physical world; for "flesh" carries one of its biblical senses, the sense of unregenerate and unsanctified corrupt ego (for example, Rom.

7:5), attached as it is to temporally bound, dead matter and con-
trasted to the free and vitally joyful Spirit, which includes the
body and the senses, as well as the Mind, Brest, Intelligence, living in the eternal Now-moment. And, on reflection, given Traherne's great desire for Felicity, for himself and for other men —
"You must Want like a GOD, that you may be Satisfied like GOD"
(*C* I 44) — the unusual, insistent tone and manner of "The Instruction" should not, after all, be altogether surprising. Nor should
Traherne's characteristic warmth, generosity, and felicity of spirit
be mistaken for passivity, weakness, or lack of firmness in the
purgative stage. There can be little doubt about Traherne's complete awareness of the value and necessity of purgation if one
carefully reads the Dobell sequence or Chapter XVII of *Christian
Ethicks,* entitled "Of Repentance. Its Original, its Nature, it is a
Purgative Vertue. Its necessity, its Excellencies," in which Traherne writes: "before a sinner can atchieve all this [Felicity], or
GOD enjoy the fruit of his Salvation, he must needs *repent,* for
Repentance is the true and substantial Preparation of the Soul, the
only Purgative Vertue, by which it is fitted for these Divine At-
tainments" (p. 128).

The words "Purer Eys" and "pure" in "The Instruction" may
remind us of the promise of the Sermon on the Mount that the
pure in heart shall see God. The end of purgation is vision, illumination and union, the nature and joy of which Traherne,
keeping the goal immediately before us, presents in "The Vision":

> The Sight
> Is Deep and Infinit;
> Ah me! tis all the Glory, Love, Light, Space,
> Joy Beauty and Varietie
> That doth adorn the Godheads Dwelling Place
> Tis all that Ey can see.   (p. 26)

The line "Order the Beauty even of Beauty is" (p. 26) gives important insight into Traherne's conception of beauty and could well serve as an internal clue to the ordered, sequential nature of the poetry. But besides being linked thematically, the poems of the Dobell Folio (like the poems of *The Temple*) are also unified and made a coherent sequence by means of recurrent words, images, symbols, especially those very major groups which we have designated. For example, in "Wonder" (l.4) and "Eden" (l.38) we read that the works of God did "crown" the child, who ("Innocence," l.58) "on the Earth did reign"; and thus we are better prepared, so to speak, for the extraordinary and paradoxical lines in "The Preparative":

> And evry Thing
> Delighted me that was their Heavnly King,   (p. 20)

and for the king symbolism of "The Vision." Moreover, just as the first and last stanzas of "The Preparative" introduce into the Dobell Folio the symbolism of the Dwelling Place, and this symbolism occurs in the first stanza of "The Vision," thereby more strongly linking the two poems together, so the Fountain symbolism in "The Vision" serves as another link between this and subsequent poems. By means of his various, interrelated and unifying images and symbols Traherne also achieves a high degree of poetic richness and complexity — and in an economic way. Discursive critical prose, which cannot duplicate such effects (except perhaps elaborately, lengthily, and, therefore, tediously) can hope to point to and discuss not all but only some instances of these poetic techniques and qualities.

Toward the end of preparing "thy Spirit," "The Vision" continues instruction as directed by the preceding poem:

First[2] then behold the World as thine, and well
    Upon the Object Dwell.
See all the Beauty of the Spacious Case,
    Lift up thy pleasd and ravisht Eys,
Admire the Glory of the Heavnly place,
    And all its Blessing prize.
That Sight well seen thy Spirit shall prepare,
    The first makes all the other Rare.   (p. 26)

Anticipating subsequent poems, especially "Love" through "Good-nesse," the last three stanzas of this poem become increasingly more ecstatic in their presentation of the nature and joy of Vision:

To see the *Fountain* is a Blessed Thing.
    It is to see the King
Of Glory face to face . . .

Who all things finds conjoynd in Him alone,
    Sees and Enjoys the Holy one.   (p. 28)

The full significance of the allusion in these lines to I Corinthians 13:12, a favorite biblical passage among mystics, becomes apparent only after we have moved through the Folio to the last poem, "Goodnesse": "For now we see through a glass, darkly; but then face to face: now I know in part; but then shall I know even as also I am known."

As vision "leads to" rapture, so "The Rapture," an ecstatic poem with a particularly Blakean last stanza, follows, is attendant upon, the ecstatic conclusion of "The Vision." After this climactic point, Traherne turns to two poems, "The Improvement" and "The Approach," which are transitional and essentially reflective. Like the "Thanksgivings for God's Attributes," "The Improvement" sings

of the tripartite Power-Wisdom-Goodness, in addition to other attributes of God, all being traditional ones which are among those
that Dionysius discusses in *The Divine Names*. Primarily, this
poem presents the central and at least implicitly pervasive idea
that the created material world would lie dead, incomplete, were
there no subject, no *Ey,* to complete, perfect, re-create it:

> But neither Goodness, Wisdom, Power, nor Love,
> Nor Happiness it self in things could be,
> Did not they all *in one fair Order* move,
> And joyntly by their Service End in *me.*
>   Had he not made an Ey to be the Sphere
>   Of all Things, none of these would e're appear.   (p. 32)

"Where man is not," Blake writes in *The Marriage of Heaven
and Hell,* "nature is barren." In Traherne's view, as in Blake's,
there is a creative, fruitful intercourse between the enlightened
man and the objective world. If the world as it is is perfect, then
an objective world uncomplemented by the subjective world would
be less than perfect. Forming a thematic chain, the complex of
ideas involved in this poem appeared in preceding poems, most
notably "The Preparative" and "The Vision," and is more fully
elucidated and expanded in "My Spirit" and in the subsequent
group of poems from "The Designe" to "Goodnesse." Again, however, the poems of the Dobell Folio are linked not only thematically but, in various ways, also stylistically and formally. For instance, among Traherne's basic, recurrent words are some which
are used also as titles of poems and which thereby help to establish a closer, tighter interrelationship among the poems. In "The
Improvement," for example, we find Rapture, Wonder, Bliss, Designe, Lov, Goodness. Because Philip omitted from F the stanza in
which Designe occurs, there is in that version less connection be-

tween and less order and direction in the poems. Even if he had kept the stanza, this would be true, for Philip changed the title "The Designe" to "The Choice."

The autobiographical element, Traherne's charting his own spiritual progress, appears most obviously in stanza 12 of "The Improvement" when Traherne, with artful "spontaneity," checks his own too rapid thematic advance:

> But Oh! the vigor of mine Infant Sence
> Drives me too far: I had not yet the Eye
> The Apprehension, or Intelligence
> Of Things so very Great Divine and High.
> But all things were *Eternal* unto me,
> And *mine,* and *Pleasing* which mine Ey did see.
>
> (p. 36)

"Eternitie, Infinity, and Lov were Silent Joys," Traherne continues in the next stanza, "All these which now our Care and Sin destroys" (p. 36), indicating that a "present" assumed voice of the poems in this middle group is that of the anxious, fallen psyche.

The first line of the next poem, "The Approach," refers directly to the joys spoken of in "The Improvement": "That Childish Thoughts such Joys inspire"; this reference is another clear, particular instance that for the sake of complete sense and comprehension the reader must take together these two poems, as indeed he must all of the poems in the variously and complexly interconnected Dobell sequence. Stanzas 2, 3, and 4 of "The Approach" then discuss at greater length the period of hardhearted alienation, of Everyman's Fall, and Traherne's own eventual conversion ("Thyself shouldst me convert I scarce know how"). Stanza 4, using singular personal pronouns rather than the plural ones of stanza 2, reads:

> Thy Gracious Motions oft in vain
> Assaulted me: My Heart did Hard remain
>   Long time: I sent my God away,
> Grievd much that he could not impart his Joy.
>   I careless was, nor did regard
> The End for which he all these Thoughts prepard.
>
> (p.38)

But inasmuch as Traherne also speaks from the perspective of redeemed vision in an achieved voice (and, representatively, insofar as he succeeds in helping to bring other men to Felicity), he can say in the fifth stanza, somewhat reminiscent of Vaughan:

> But now with New and Open Eys,   25
> I see beneath as if above the Skies;
>   And as I Backward look again,
> See all his Thoughts and mine most Clear and Plain.   28
>
> (p. 38)

And in the next recapitulative stanza, echoing "From Dust I rise, And out of Nothing now awake" ("The Salutation," p. 6), he reveals his "present" joyful vision and estate:

> From Nothing taken first I was,   31
> What Wondrous Things his Glory brought to pass!
>   Now in this World I him behold,
> And me enveloped in more then Gold;
>   In deep Abysses of Delights,
> In present Hidden Precious Benefits.   36
>
> (p. 38)

"The Approach," then, employing a twofold perspective or double voice, moves from the speaker's childhood joys, through a long period of indifferent and hardhearted "Apostasie," to a present Felicity, a progression that reflects the fundamental, overall pattern of Creation-Fall-Redemption in the Dobell Folio.

I have numbered the lines just quoted from stanzas 5 and 6 so that they might be more readily compared to Philip's version:

> But now with new and open Eys 25
> I see beneath as if abov the Skies:
> When I on what is past reflect
> His Thoughts and Mine I plainly recollect: 28
>
> From Nothing taken first I was: 31
> What wondrous things His Goodness brought to pass!
> Now in this World I Him discern,
> And what His Dealings with me meant I learn,
> He sow'd in me Seeds of Delights
> That might grow up to future Benefits. 36

(p. 39)

Not only does Philip lose the possible reminiscence of Vaughan in Thomas' line 27, but Philip's lines also are abstract, flat, and prosaic by contrast to the original, and tend to blunt and "mentalize" Thomas' direct seeing and direct pointing. For example, Thomas' "look," "See," and "behold" become "reflect," "recollect," and "discern" ("behold," incidentally, appears frequently in the Psalms and "discern" does not appear at all). Philip considerably diminishes if not totally silences Thomas' achieved voice, his present Benefits, which are "Hidden" only to worldly-wise, unredeemed eyes. Literal-minded Philip apparently had little appreciation for paradox, irony, complexity, and biblical, contemplative terminology and ideas, whereas in lines 35–36 Thomas uses the traditional "Abysses" and perhaps had in mind an idea like Augustine's "For Thou hid-dest these things from the wise, and revealedst them to babes," [3] or the biblical "In whom are hid all the treasures of wisdom and knowledge" and "your life is hid with Christ in God" (Col. 2:3, 3:3), verses which he quotes in *C* IV 4. Philip's changes destroy the poetry, the art and thought, of Thomas' lines and plainly reveal some of the profound differences between a nervous versifier and a joyful poet-mystic, such as the vital difference between moralistically deferring Felicity to some remote never-never future rather than mystically realizing Felicity in the present Now-moment, the only "time" that truly is.

Just as the first stanza of "The Approach" refers to the joys spoken of at the end of "The Improvement," so the last stanza points to the subject of following poems:

> Childhood might it self alone be said,
>   My Tutor, Teacher, Guid to be,
> Instructed then even by the Deitie.   (p. 40)

These lines echo and further answer the earlier call for "Instruction." Because childhood, the period which corresponds to the prelapsarian state, is common to every man's experience and is like unto Redemption, the direction and end of the Dobell Folio, the next eight poems, "Dumnesse" to "Speed," develop more fully the instructive answer, the meaning of childhood for man's fallen condition, with particular emphasis on the excellence and wisdom of Nature and the natural or Edenic estate of the very young, as-yet-uncorrupted child. Rather than continuing in the tone of "The Instruction" by employing a hell-fire-and-brimstone manner to excoriate fallen man and angrily exhort him to repent, Traherne chooses instead to teach by giving a positive sense of the nature of Felicity, by revealing the full significance of felicitous childhood, of a lost or hidden but recoverable identity. He seems to have known that the less he "preaches," the better he will be heard; the more genuinely poetic his poetry is, the more readily will insight into the true nature of Felicity be realized. While frequently reminding the reader of the Fall and of every man's fall, Traherne chooses, in other words, the much more meaningful and effective emphasis and strategy.

That Traherne uses words with the precision of a poet, that his catalogs, his appositive and cumulative techniques, do not mean any plain word will do as well as another, may be further illustrated by our considering the opening lines of "Dumnesse":

> Sure Man was born to Meditat on Things,
> And to Contemplat the Eternal Springs
> Of God and Nature, Glory, Bliss and Pleasure;
> That Life and Love might be his Heavnly Treasure:
> And therfore Speechless made at first, that he
> Might in himself profoundly Busied be.   (p. 40)

The words Meditat and Contemplat follow immediately upon "The Approach," the poem which first introduces the very important word thoughts into the sequence and which is centrally concerned with "Childish Thoughts." Furthermore, in the opening lines of "Dumnesse" Traherne is not merely repetitious. Although mystical writers sometimes use the terms interchangeably, they also often distinguish between meditation and contemplation. In *Benjamin Major,* Richard of St. Victor, following Hugh of St. Victor, offers these definitions: "Contemplation is the clear and free glance of the soul bearing intently upon objects of perception, to its furthest limits. Meditation, however, is an industrious attention of the mind concentrated diligently upon the investigation of some object." And he distinguishes between their modes of operating: "Meditation with great mental industry, plods along the steep and laborious road keeping the end in view. Contemplation on a free wing, circles around with great nimbleness wherever the impulse takes it . . . it is the property of contemplation to adhere with wonder to the object which brings it joy." [4] "Things" is not just a rhyme word for "Springs." Meditation is discursive, rational, ideological, and therefore has quite precisely to do with "Things." Contemplation is imaginative, intuitive, and therefore has directly and aptly to do with the No-Thing, Godhead, or, in Traherne's exact phrasing, "the Eternal Springs of God and Nature, Glory, Bliss, and Pleasure."

The young child, in whom conceptualization is undeveloped, is directly, intuitively aware of and in communion with the Godhead. Thus, as "Dumnesse" reads, he can "see all Creatures full of Deities; Especially Ones self" (lines which Philip deleted) and is "Pleasd with all that God hath done" (p. 42). As the child acquires language and develops his conceptual powers, he begins to grow out of his intuitive awareness of the Source of all things. (Quite pertinently, lines 9–16 of "Dumnesse" are richly connotative of the Fall, lines 67–88 of the speaker's own Fall; and the opening lines of the correlative "Silence" refer explicitly to "the Fall" and "Adam.") The child is educated, learns the customs of his adult society, begins to become an ego and to see conventionally, and thereby loses the vision of the holiness and divinity of "all Creatures." The thinking and naming of the "I who feeds on notions and words" makes things seem to exist where, before, all was No-thing. As the child is conditioned to see the unbounded as bounded, his developing, conceptualizing intellect, necessary and useful though it is, divides this from that, "Thou" from "that," and distinguishes as other what in actuality is nondual, indivisible, inextricably interrelated and interdependent.

From a larger perspective, however, the Fall is both necessary and fortunate. This traditional, orthodox, though strangely para-

doxical idea, which implies no denial of free will, is stated most
clearly and succinctly in the *Exultet,* a hymn from the Roman
Catholic liturgy for Holy Saturday: "O certe necessarium Adae
peccatum, quod Christi morte deletum est! O felix culpa, quae
talem ac tantum meruit habere Redemptorem!" Apart from this
source, which was in liturgical use as early as the seventh and
possibly as early as the fourth century, Traherne could have found
various expressions of the idea in such writers as Ambrose, Greg-
ory the Great, Wyclif, Francis de Sales, and Du Bartas, among
others.[5] Understanding the biblical pattern of Creation-Fall-Redemption not only in the historical, literal sense but also in a
mythic way, Traherne sees every man truly as Adam (*C* I 75, II 12,
for example) and holds, thus, that the Fall in the mythic sense is
the godlike child's growing up, becoming "civilized," "human,"
being corrupted by others, whose "Corruption Derived from Adam
. . . I was ten thousand times more prone to Good and Excellent
Things, then evil. But I was quickly tainted and fell by others"
(*C* III 8). The progress of each individual from infancy to adulthood spiritually recapitulates the fall of the race in Adam. Traherne, let us emphasize, nowhere repudiates the Fall in its historic
sense. But, thoroughgoing Christian that he is, one of his distinctions lies in his giving, in the *Centuries* and poems especially, extended, meaningful treatment to the Fall in its mythic sense as
well; understood in this way the Fall is not just ancient "history"
but also a poetic account of the psychological and spiritual facts of
every human life. To pass from innocence to the thousand times
more fortunate, blessed redeemed state ("the state of Glory") and
actually and fully realize the life of pneuma, one's Divine Sonship,
every man must move through "the state of Trial," must grow up
in every sense of the phrase.

"IF any man be disposed to cavil further, and to urge, that GOD
might at the very first have placed Angels and Men in the state of

Glory, the Reply is at hand: that GOD very well understandeth the beauty of Proportion, that Harmony and Symmetry springs from a variety of excellent Things in several places, fitly answering to, and perfecting each other: that the state of Trial, and the state of Glory are so mysterious in their Relation, that neither without the other could be absolutely perfect: Innumerable Beauties would be lost, and many transcendent Vertues and Perfections be abolished, with the estate of Trial, if that had been laid aside, the continual appearance and effect of which is to enrich and beautifie the King-dom of GOD everlastingly" (*CE*, p. 184). Clearly, without the Fall and our consequent state of trial God's universe would be less than perfect and man less than fully blessed. "If you ask, what is becom of us since the Fall? becaus all these things now lately named seem to pertain to the Estate of Innocency; Truly Now we have superadded Treasures: Jesus Christ . . . GOD is more Delightfull then He was in Eden. Then he was as Delightfull as was possible but he had not that occasion, as by Sin was offered, to superad many more Delights then before. Being more Delightfull and more Amiable, He is more Desirable and may now be more Easily yea Strongly Beloved. for the Amiableness of the Object Enables us to lov it" (*C* IV 53). The Fall, though lamentable in itself, is, in this larger view with its overriding and subsuming considerations of Beauty, Joy, and Love, the necessary and ulti-mately fortunate means to a still greater end. As in *Paradise Lost* (XII, 469–478), all the evil is to serve and to be turned finally to Good in this life of the open-eyed, all-comprehending redeemed man as in the afterlife of the saved (see *CE*, p. 101).

Perhaps another, specific reason why the Fall may be considered fortunate is that language, a cause of our Fall, is also a means for bringing us closer to Redemption. Thus, Traherne speaks in the *Third Century* of the usefulness of his university studies, effected largely in and through language, and his study of the Bible, which took him a great distance along the spiritual path; and thus, also, the contemplatives advise study and prayer as serving a useful preparatory role prior to the infusion of divine grace — which comes always from God, not through man's efforts. The wind bloweth where it listeth.

Traherne's position in "Dumnesse" and elsewhere must not be oversimplified as mere anti-intellectualism. "Ignorance" may paradoxically be "learned and happy" for the unfallen child, but it is not so for the fallen adult. Yet rational knowledge is not sufficient for attaining Felicity. As we read in the "Select Meditations," "Knowledg is a rare Accomplishment, and they who undervalue it betray their want of it, for it hath no Enemy but Ignorance. Yet is it not a Star of the first magnitude nor the one Thing needfull." In a striking analogy, Traherne says it is as St. John the Baptist was to Christ, and he continues: "Grace and vertue must carry us to Heaven . . . Bare knowledge gives no man a Title to Heavenly Joys: It is the Light onely in which they are Enjoyed" (IV, 22). And if we attend carefully to the opening sections of the *Centuries* IV, we should not misunderstand Traherne: "Since no man therefore can be a Man, unless he be a Philosopher, nor a true Philosopher unless he be a Christian, nor a Perfect Christian unless he be a Divine; evry man ought to spend his time, in studying diligently Divine Philosophy" (*C* IV 3). And we should see more clearly the significance of the analogy involving the Baptist and Christ: "Jesus Christ is the Wisdom of the father" (*C* IV 4). "And sure it is the Essence of a Christian or very near it to be a Lover of Wisdom" (*C* IV 5). "Wherfore Get Wisdom, and with all thy Getting get understanding" (*C* IV 7; see also *CE* chs. V, VIII–X, and p. 184).

In regarding Christ, pneuma, as Sophia or Wisdom, the Word by whom the "very good" universe is eternally created, Traherne follows ancient biblical and mystical tradition; and more particularly, like such other Renaissance English poets as Spenser, Donne, and Milton, he writes from within the complex Renaissance tradition of Wisdom, of sapientia versus scientia.[6] "The Improvement," "Nature," "Ease," "The Enquirie," "Amendment," and "Thoughts" III and IV, the last four poems being in the Redemption group, refer overtly to "Wisdom," usually in conjunction with images of creation, incarnation, or light. "Dumnesse," which primarily concerns the meaning of original childhood for fallen man, reads,

> No Ear,
> But Eys them selvs were all the Hearers there.
> And evry Stone, and Evry Star a Tongue,
> And evry Gale of Wind a Curious Song.
> The Heavens were an Orakle, and spake
> *Divinity:* The Earth did undertake
> The office of a Priest; And I being Dum
> (Nothing besides was dum;) All things did com
> With Voices and Instructions; but when I
> Had gaind a Tongue, their Power began to die.
> Mine Ears let other Noises in, not theirs;
> A Nois Disturbing all my Songs and Prayers.
> My foes puld down the Temple to the Ground,
> They my Adoring Soul did deeply Wound,
> And casting that into a Swoon, destroyd
> The Oracle, and all I there enjoyd.   (pp. 42, 44)

To get Wisdom is to raise up the Temple again, to become like unto a child, who is not "depraved with Tongues,"

> Nor Injurd by the Errors and the Wrongs
> That *Mortal Words* convey.   (p. 40)

It is to acquire and use but transcend ordinary knowledge and its vehicle, language, to attain to the life of pneuma, to hear and "see" again in the silence the Word of God.

Paradoxically, then, by language, one of man's highest abilities and that which most distinguishes him as a civilized human creature, man falls from Felicity: "I then my Bliss did, when my Silence, break" (p. 40). Yet still more paradoxically, by language and intellect, by reading Scripture, by meditating through language on things, man may be lead back *toward* the Eternal Springs and, ultimately, be truly and fully civilized. "Therefore that he may raise," reads one of Donne's famous Hymns, "the Lord throws down." For Dante, the way out of Hell is through the center; and Virgil, who stands for reason and language, among other things, can lead Dante through Hell and up Mount Purgatory, but he cannot lead him into Eden nor into Paradise. The psyche itself, then, is to a degree instrumental in its own regeneration. Indeed, what it most essentially learns is its own incapacity to effect Felicity, salvation. He who would save his life shall lose it; he who loses his life, gives up the egoistic struggle, wholly admits, that is, his total dependence on God and discovers God's nearness, attains to Wisdom and lives in the mode of Eternal Life.

The Bliss consequent upon the child's silence and his "learned and . . . Happy Ignorance" points a way for the wandering fallen adult in "Silence":

> A quiet Silent Person may possess
> All that is Great or High in Blessedness.
> The Inward Work is the Supreme: for all
> The other were occasiond by the Fall. (p. 44)

Continuing his theme of childhood in terms of the central biblical myth and developing the pneuma-psyche distinction, Traherne distinguishes the inward man's supreme work, "which Adam in his Innocence Performed" (p. 44), from "These outward Busy Acts," which "he knew not" and which "were Things of a Second or a lower Sphere" (p. 46). This poem's heroic couplets, its allusions to the fallen state (lines 3–4, 9–20, 53–60), and its important contemplative theme of silence and "wise passiveness" strongly connect it technically and thematically to "Dumnesse," while its extended symbolism relates it back to "The Preparative" and especially to "The Vision" and forward to numerous other poems. The last two dozen lines of "Silence" display some of the poem's Fountain, King, and Sphere symbolism:

> In that fair World one only was the Friend,
> One Golden Stream, one Spring, one only End.
> There only one did Sacrifice and Sing
> To only one Eternal Heavenly King.
> The Union was so Strait between them two,
> That all was eithers which my Soul could view.
> His Gifts, and my Possessions, both our Treasures;
> He mine, and I the Ocean of his Pleasures.
> He was an Ocean of Delights from Whom
> The Living Springs and Golden Streams did com:
> My Bosom was an Ocean into which
> They all did run. And me they did enrich.
> A vast and Infinit Capacitie,
> Did make my Bosom like the Deitie,
> In Whose Mysterious and Celestial Mind
> All Ages and all Worlds together shind.
> Who tho he nothing said did always reign,
> And in Himself Eternitie contain.

The World was more in me, then I in it.
The King of Glory in my Soul did sit.
And to Himself in me he always gave,
All that he takes Delight to see me have.
For so my Spirit was an Endless Sphere,
Like God himself, and Heaven and Earth was there.

(pp. 48, 50)

The reference to "my Spirit" and the Sphere symbolism in the penultimate line of "Silence," not to mention previous key words like "Friend" and "shind" and certain continued central ideas, lead directly to the poem "My Spirit," the stanzaic and poetic complexity of which is exactly correlative to Traherne's brilliant, sustained effort in this poem to reveal the meaning of pneuma. About "My Spirit" Margoliouth writes: "This is Traherne's most comprehensive poem. It contains the experience of the Infant Eye reflected on in maturity, the mature experience of the Infant Eye regained, the mature man's mystical inner experience, and all three united in an act of the understanding which is itself a further experience" (II, 349). This extraordinary but critically neglected poem makes unusual demands on the reader and presents the critic with a considerable task. Although we need not attempt as complete and detailed an analysis as we gave to "The Preparative," it will be useful to our discussion to have the full text before us.

My Spirit

I

My Naked Simple Life was I.
    That Act so Strongly Shind
Upon the Earth, the Sea, the Skie,

That was the Substance of My Mind.
    The Sence it self was I.   5
I felt no Dross nor Matter in my Soul,
No Brims nor Borders, such as in a Bowl
We see, My Essence was Capacitie.
            That felt all Things,
                The Thought that Springs   10
Therfrom's it self. It hath no other Wings
    To Spread abroad, nor Eys to see,
        Nor Hands Distinct to feel,
        Nor Knees to Kneel:
But being Simple like the Deitie   15
    In its own Centre is a Sphere
    Not shut up here, but evry Where.

                        2

    It Acts not from a Centre to
        Its Object as remote,
    But present is, when it doth view,   20
    Being with the Being it doth note.
        Whatever it doth do,
It doth not by another Engine work,
But by it self; which in the Act doth lurk.
Its Essence is Transformed into a true   25
            And perfect Act.
            And so Exact
Hath God appeard in this Mysterious Fact,
    That tis all Ey, all Act, all Sight,
        And what it pleas can be,   30
            Not only see,
Or do; for tis more Voluble then Light:
    Which can put on ten thousand Forms,
    Being clothd with what it self adorns.

3

This made me present evermore   35
    With whatso ere I saw.
An Object, if it were before
My Ey, was by Dame Natures Law,
    Within my Soul. Her Store
Was all at once within me; all her Treasures   40
Were my Immediat and Internal Pleasures,
Substantial Joys, which did inform my Mind.
    With all she wrought,
    My Soul was fraught,
And evry Object in my Soul a Thought   45
    Begot, or was; I could not tell,
    Whether the Things did there
    Themselvs appear,
Which in my Spirit *truly* seemd to dwell;
    Or whether my conforming Mind   50
    Were not alone even all that shind.

4

But yet of this I was most sure,
    That at the utmost Length,
(so Worthy was it to endure)
My Soul could best Express its Strength.   55
    It was Indivisible, and so Pure,
That all my Mind was wholy Evry where
What ere it saw, twas ever wholy there;
The Sun ten thousand Legions off, was nigh:
    The utmost Star,   60
    Tho seen from far,
Was present in the Apple of my Eye.
    There was my Sight, my Life, my Sence,

My Substance and my Mind
        My Spirit Shind   65
Even there, not by a Transeunt Influence.
    The Act was Immanent, yet there.
    The Thing remote, yet felt even here.

5

O Joy! O Wonder, and Delight!
        O Sacred Mysterie!   70
My Soul a Spirit infinit!
An Image of the Deitie!
        A pure Substantiall Light!
That Being Greatest which doth Nothing seem!
Why twas my All, I nothing did esteem   75
But that alone. A Strange Mysterious Sphere!
        A Deep Abyss
        That sees and is
The only Proper Place or Bower of Bliss.
    To its Creator tis so near   80
        In Lov and Excellence
        In Life and Sence,
In Greatness Worth and Nature; And so Dear;
    In it, without Hyperbole,
    The Son and friend of God we see.   85

6

A Strange Extended Orb of Joy,
    Proceeding from within,
Which did on evry side convey
It self, and being nigh of Kin
        To God did evry Way   90
Dilate it self even in an Instant, and

Like an Indivisible Centre Stand
At once Surrounding all Eternitie.
   Twas not a sphere
    Yet did appear   95
One infinit. Twas somwhat evry where.
  And tho it had a Power to see
    Far more, yet still it shind
     And was a Mind
Exerted for it saw Infinitie   100
  Twas not a Sphere, but twas a Power
  Invisible, and yet a Bower.

7

  O Wondrous Self! O Sphere of Light,
    O Sphere of Joy most fair;
  O Act, O Power infinit;   105
  O Subtile, and unbounded Air!
    O Living Orb of Sight!
Thou which within me art, yet Me! Thou Ey,
And Temple of his Whole Infinitie!
O what a World art Thou! a World within!   110
    All Things appear,
    All Objects are
Alive in thee! Supersubstancial, Rare,
  Abov them selvs, and nigh of Kin
    To those pure Things we find   115
    In his Great Mind
Who made the World! tho now Ecclypsd by Sin.
  There they are Usefull and Divine,
  Exalted there they ought to Shine.

         (pp. 50, 52, 54, 56)

Generally speaking, the logical structure of this poem is "inductive," moving from analysis to conclusion, as opposed, let us say, to the "deductive" structure of "The Preparative," which advances from its first two stanzas' poetic statements about the infant's body and soul to development and elaboration in its subsequent stanzas. The first four stanzas of "My Spirit" are more expository and analytical and as such lead to the last three stanzas, which are more ecstatic and appositive. Most, though by no means all, of the poem's pneuma-revealing symbolism occurs in the conclusive last three stanzas; that is, by design the poem is intended to lead us to greater insight into the meaning and nature of Spirit. Traherne's first three major classes of biblical, mystical symbols — Eye, Sphere, Sun — predominate by far, and these appropriately are imagistically closely interrelated. To a lesser extent, the Dwelling Place and Mirror groups are also represented.

Several other formal and stylistic points deserve specific comment. Immediately, in the opening words Naked and Simple, as well as elsewhere in the poem, we recognize some of the characteristic terminology of the contemplatives, as when Eckhart writes of the redeemed man that "he lives where the Father lives; that is, in simplicity and in nakedness of being." [7] In the first stanza, Traherne uses a literal, cumulative catalog (Wings, Eys, Hands, Knees of lines 11–14) to indicate what pneuma is not; by contrast, in the second stanza, as indeed throughout the poem, he uses a symbolic, appositive catalog ("tis all Ey, all Act, all Sight," line 29) to suggest what pneuma is. As pointed out in Chapter Two, the literal, cumulative catalog is usually denotative of the "visible" external world and the symbolic, appositive catalog is usually connotative of the "invisible" inner essential man. "My Spirit" will go on to suggest that in an ultimate sense the intellectual distinction between outer and inner is not operative, that object and subject, finally and rightly understood, are nondual. "The Sence itself was I" is a most succinct single expression of this extremely difficult mystical idea (difficult to understand and to explain). This idea is in large part developed through Traherne's echoic, symbolic, and accumulative biblical technique, which is apparent, for example, in the way that the first and sixth lines of this poem resonate with lines 20 and 42–44, respectively, of "The Preparative":

> A Naked Simple Pure *Intelligence*   (p. 20)

> Not prepossest with Dross,
> Nor stifly glued to gross
> And dull Materials that might ruine me,   (p. 22)

and in the way that the first four lines of "My Spirit," especially line 3, recall this literal catalog from "The Salutation":

> The Earth, the Seas, the Light, the Day, the Skies,
> The Sun and Stars are mine; if those I prize.   (p. 6)

Whereas "The Salutation" articulates the more accessible idea of the necessity of prizing for the sake of true possession, "The Preparative" and "My Spirit" express the profounder idea that the single-eyed, undivided, unfallen or redeemed Self truly is at one with the world he creatively and fully appreciates. The Dobell poems do not of course baldly assert this most difficult concept. Rather, by means of different symbols and poetic techniques, the careful "critical peruser" gradually, subtly, repeatedly, variously "discovers" and thereby more fully and deeply actually realizes this idea and its development in the whole sequence.

Since "My Spirit" concerns "beginnings" and creation in a special sense, I would suggest that a particularly helpful context in which to read this rich poem is Genesis 1, John 1, and Eckhart's

masterpiece, *Commentary on the Gospel according to St. John.*[8]
In his short Prologue to this work, Eckhart reminds us that in
Book VII of the *Confessions* Augustine says he read "a great part
of this first chapter of John's Gospel in the works of Plato."[9]
Throughout his *Commentary,* Eckhart quotes and alludes to
Augustine more frequently than he does any other writer; Aristotle is the second most frequently cited author. In the first words
of Chapter I, Eckhart draws our attention to the parallel between
Genesis 1 and John 1: "It must be pointed out in the first place
that this very statement, 'In the beginning was the Word, and the
Word was with God,' and several of the ensuing statements are
contained in the words: 'And God said, let there be light: and
there was light. And God saw the light, that it was good, and He
separated the light and the darkness' (Genesis 1, 3–4)."[10] "My
Spirit" is a Neoplatonic poem, but more precisely it is a Christian,
biblical Neoplatonic poem, and the context just suggested (as
opposed, say, to an exclusively or predominantly Neoplatonic one)
provides, I believe, the various religious and philosophic elements
of Traherne's thought, including the Aristotelian elements, essentially in their proper and just proportions. Unless we have some
idea of how a contemplative, like Eckhart, who was familiar with
the Church Fathers and classical philosophy, read Genesis 1 and
John 1, we cannot, I think, fully understand and appreciate "My
Spirit."

   To speak generally, the poem "My Spirit" explains further, in
its own unique and distinctive way, the meaning of pneuma primarily by articulating and developing the idea that unfallen and
redeemed activity are perfectly "imitative" of God's creative
activity through his Word as expressed by Genesis 1 and John 1
— providing we understand those biblical texts in an Eckhartian
and Augustinian sense, a sense consistent with Traherne's other
works. The main concepts found at length in the prose *Centuries,*

II 40–46, 73–91, III 62–68, and IV 4 have been distilled, refined, and economically and poetically expressed in "My Spirit." It should at once be made explicit that on one level, let us say the literal level, Genesis 1, John 1, and "My Spirit" concern different matters: Genesis 1 is about God's creation of the world at the beginning of time; John 1 is about the unique Word or Son of God, who was with God, and who was God, and who in the beginning made all things and then at some later time entered the world; "My Spirit" is primarily about the beginning or childhood of the speaker, his creative vision, who he truly was and who, redeemed, he truly is. But on the poetic or mythic level, this poem makes it clear that the speaker or, more precisely, his essential Self is "without Hyperbole, The Son and friend of God," and that this divine Spirit "makes" or "re-makes" the otherwise dead material world in the eternal Now-moment, for "evry Moments Preservation is a New Creation" (*C* II 91). As the Son of God, he willingly does the joyful work of God, sustaining or re-creating God's very good works, the universe, which wise work is also truly play — Wisdom, as it were, playing before the throne of God.

The two major relationships of the poem are those of *my Spirit* to God and of *my Spirit* to the so-called external world, the "Material World" which in itself "is Dead and feeleth Nothing" (*C* II 90). These relationships are complex and paradoxical in that *my Spirit* is both identical and not identical with God, and identical and not identical with the external world which it quickens. Throughout the poem Traherne maintains this delicate balance of distinguishable but ultimately indivisible natures. Eckhart's commentary on the Word and its relationships to God and the world provides the contemplative context which helps to explicate the relationships of *my Spirit* to God and the world. Indeed, Eckhart's last sentence in the following lengthy passage invites and justifies our procedure:

We have, accordingly, four considerations, namely that the thing issuing is in the producer, that it is in it as the seed is in its source, as the word is in the speaker, and that it is in it as the idea, in which and through which the product issues from the producer.

In the fifth place, however, we must realize that by the very fact of a thing's issuing from something else it is distinguished from it. Hence follows the statement: 'The Word was with God'. It does not say 'below God', nor 'it came down from God', but 'the Word was with God'. For the expression 'with God' indicates a certain measure of equality. In this connexion it should be noted that in analogical relations the product is always inferior, less, more imperfect than, and unequal to the producer, whereas in homogeneous relations it is always equal to it, not sharing the same nature but receiving it in its totality, simply and integrally and on an equal footing, from its principle.

Hence, sixthly, that which issues forth is the 'son' of the producer. For a son is one who becomes another in respect of personality but not other in nature.

From this it follows, seventhly, that the son or the word is identical with the father or principle. And so we have next: 'The Word was God'. Yet here it must be noted that, although the product in analogical relations derives from the producer, it is nevertheless below its principle, not with it. Furthermore, it is other in nature and so is not the principle itself. Yet in so far as it is in the latter, it is not other in nature nor yet in substance. A chest in the mind of an artist is not a chest but the life and intelligence of the artist, his actual concept. My purpose in mentioning this point is to bring out the implication contained in these words on the procession of the divine Persons, namely, that the same thing holds good and is found in the procession and production of every being in nature and in art.[11]

Eckhart's terms producer, product, and issuing (which suggest Neoplatonic emanationism[12]) are parallel to Traherne's distinction in stanza 4 between a "Transeunt Influence" and an "Immanent" Act and to Traherne's "Proceeding" and "Dilate" of stanza 6. In Eckhart, the Word is the product whch issues from God, the producer; and the world (as later passages in Eckhart make still clearer) is the product which issues from the Word or Son, the producer, for "All things were made by him" (John 1:3). Similarly in Traherne's poem, *my Spirit* is the product which issues from "its Creator" to which it is "so near . . . In Greatness Worth and Nature" (lines 80–83); and the "World within" (which paradoxically is also the world without — see lines 35–40 in particular) is the product of the creative spirit acting upon the material world. Most notably, the relationship between the Word and God (that is, the Word's being identical with but distinguishable from God) that Eckhart painstakingly describes is essentially the same relationship between *my Spirit* and God that Traherne carefully but also poetically describes throughout the poem and perhaps most clearly in stanza 5, the first of the three conclusive stanzas. Throughout the poem, Traherne distinguishes *my Spirit* from God, but also indicates that it is "nigh of Kin To" and "like the Deitie"; he applies traditonal symbols for God to *my Spirit,* and ascribes to *my Spirit* attributes, such as infinity, which are traditional attributes of God. Just as God is, so the true Self or pneuma is all Act, all Spirit, and

> being Simple like the Deitie
> In its own Centre is a Sphere
> Not shut up here, but evry Where.

Writing on the nature of Being, St. Bonaventure concludes that because Being is "most simple and greatest [see also line 74: "That Being Greatest which doth Nothing seem!"], therefore it is entirely within and entirely without all things and, therefore, is an intelligible sphere whose center is everywhere and whose circumference nowhere." [13] There can be no doubt as to Traherne's meaning and his full awareness of it, when we compare his "Thanksgivings for God's Attributes": "O the wonderful excellency of thine eternal Nature! It is as a Sphere, O Lord, into which we were born, whose Centre is everywhere, circumference no where" (p. 318; and see *C* II 80).

The speaker's essential being, then, is an Act which consists in the full realization of its eternal and infinite potentialities, an eternal and infinite Act. In Traherne's day, the word Act had the now obsolete senses of both Reality and Active Principle (OED). Like the God of Aristotle and the Scholastics, *my Spirit* is pure Actuality, Thought-Thinking-Thought: "The Thought that Springs Therfrom's it self." (We read in the first stanza of "Thoughts I" that Thoughts are the "Machines Great Which in my Spirit God did Seat" — p. 169 — which interrelates the "Thoughts" poems with "My Spirit.") In stanzas 1 and 3 of "My Spirit" Thought, the spiritual connection (so to speak) between God and the world, is contemplative or noetic and creative, not meditative, abstract, or rational; can be either sensuous or nonsensuous; and corresponds to Eckhart's "idea" in the lengthy passage cited above and, with qualification, to the Platonic Idea. (Nor should this be surprising, for it is precisely in his conception of God that Aristotle is closest to Platonism.) Later in his *Commentary,* Eckhart cites Augustine on the Greek *logos* signifying in Latin *idea* (that is, *ratio*) as well as *word,* and then goes on to clarify what he means by "idea":

it should be noted that 'idea' is taken in a double sense. For there is the idea received or abstracted by the intellect from things, the idea in this case being subsequent to the things from which it is abstracted. There is also an idea which is prior to things, the cause and idea of the things, which is indicated by the definition and is grasped by the intellect in the innermost ground of the things themselves. The latter is the idea now under discussion. Therefore it is said that the logos, that is, the idea, is in the beginning. 'In the beginning', he says, 'was the Word'.[14]

Like Eckhart's "idea," Traherne's "Thought" is neither discursive nor abstract. We saw in our discussion of "The Preparative" that Traherne holds, with Plotinus and others, that discursive thought cannot apprehend God, the absolutely simple. Now, it is very important to realize also that, for Traherne, the mystic or Felicitous experience does not involve or consist of ideas "received or abstracted by the intellect from things." Since there is a tendency in some non-Christian Neoplatonists toward rationalistic abstraction — or at least their articulation of the matter has been interpreted as such — we must here make some careful distinctions concerning extrovertive, sensuous mysticism and introvertive nonsensuous mysticism. Traherne writes of and apparently enjoyed both kinds, as also we saw in "The Preparative." In "My Spirit," both kinds again seem to obtain, but extrovertive mysticism, particularly involving the sense of sight, clearly predominates. When mystics write of not being able to apprehend ultimate reality with the bodily, fleshy, or conventional eyes or senses (*C* II 76, "Innocence," line 16, and "Thoughts I," stanzas 6–7, for example) they are referring to either (1) nonsensuous introvertive mysticism or (2) the necessity of purgation so that the veil of custom and selfish solicitude will be removed, so that eventually one may sensuously perceive ultimate reality with a pure heart through cleansed senses. In *The City of God,* St. Augustine writes: "Thus, it was with 'heart' that the Prophet says he saw . . . Now just think, when God will be 'all in all,' how much greater will be this gift of vision in the hearts of all! The eyes of the body will still retain their function and will be found where they now are, and the spirit, through its spiritual body, will make use of the eyes." [15] This is the kind of creative and apocalyptic vision that Traherne writes of in "My Spirit" and elsewhere, when God in the eternal Now-moment is all in all, when Christ or pneuma in us sees. He does not mean seeing objects in some generalized, rationalistic, abstract way. This, I believe, ultimately comes to thinking about objects rather than actually looking at them with the heart through the eyes. As I understand him, Traherne means seeing with fully open eyes rather than with closed or indifferent eyes; or seeing felicitously into the particular-universal suchness or quiddity of an object with regenerated or enlightened heart and eyes rather than seeing in such a way as mentally to abstract an "essence" from the object, as if essence and object could ever really (that is, in fact, not just in mind) be dualistically separated.[16]

That Traherne's Spirit or Thought, like Eckhart's *Logos* and idea, is, among its other meanings, essentially a Christ-like creative Act and all that is "made" through this active, creative power (the product being, in some important sense, in the prior, causing producer, or, putting it another way, "so is the Soul Transformed into the Being of its Object" — *C* II 78) becomes most apparent by stanza 3 of "My Spirit." [17] Noting that stanza 3 ends on the word "shind," a key biblical word [18] in the sequence, a word that, echoing "shineth" in John 1:5, practically opens the poem, occurs repeatedly, and then literally closes the poem, we again have recourse to Eckhart's elucidating remarks: "Indeed, it would be more correct to say that in the case of created things nothing 'shines' but their ideas . . . The idea, then, is 'the light shining in darkness' — that is to say in created things — yet not enclosed, intermingled or comprehended by it." [19] Eckhart then concludes:

We can see then how this passage, from 'in the beginning was the Word' down to 'There was a man sent from God', may be expounded by means of the ideas and properties of natural things. It is clear too that the actual words of the Evangelist, if subjected to careful scrutiny, teach us about the nature and properties of things whether in being or in operation and so in addition to establishing our faith provide us with instruction on the nature of things. For the Son of God Himself, 'the Word in the beginning', is the idea, 'a sort of creative power charged with all living and immutable ideas, which are all one in it', as Augustine says in the last chapter of Book vi of his *De Trinitate*. [20]

In the opening of the first stanza we read that in the beginning of the speaker's life the Act (which is "the Substance of My Mind," is "My Spirit") "so Strongly Shind Upon the Earth, the Sea, the Skie." Having in mind Traherne's conception of pure vision and the principle "That evry Moments Preservation is a New Creation" (*C* II 91), this is tantamount to, as Genesis 1 puts it, the creation or re-creation "in the beginning" of "the heaven and the earth," to the moving of "the Spirit of God . . . upon the face of the waters," and to the letting there be light. Considering stanza 3, especially the alternatives presented by lines 45–51, "That Act" is also tantamount to, as John 1 puts it, "in the beginning . . . all things" being "made by him," in whom is "the life" which is "the light of men," the light which "shineth in darkness." ("My Naked Simple Life was I," "My Spirit Shind," "A pure Substantial

Light!" are some of the biblically resonant lines of the poem, lines
which are particularly echoic of those words in John 1 that are
associated with or symbolic of Christ.) This creative Act is, in
other words, "a repetition in the finite mind of the eternal act of
creation in the infinite I am"; for the pure vision of which Traherne and the contemplatives speak is, I believe, comparable to
Coleridge's view of the imagination. Like Traherne, Coleridge
conceives of objects in themselves as essentially fixed and dead;
the imagination, essentially vital, is the God-like faculty in man,
"the living Power and prime Agent of all human Perception." [21]

Some additional comments on and examples of Traherne's poetic
use of echoic, symbolic, plurisignificant, appositive, and paradoxical
language should serve further to enhance our appreciation of his
art as well as further to expound and clarify his meaning. Focusing on that most interesting stanza 3, we note that "Substantial" and "inform" in the line "Substantial Joys, which did inform
my Mind" carry a double meaning. Similarly, "conforming Mind"
is precisely plurisignificant: (1) a mind which shapes or creates the
world, and (2) a mind that conforms to God, of whom it is an
image, in imitating, so to speak, his creative activity. "And evry
Object in my Soul a Thought Begot, or was" is an admirably
exact, economic syntactical ambiguity; and the prepositional phrase
"in my Soul" (the Soul being "wholy Evry where") modifies both
"Object" and "Thought." We should take the several sets of alternatives in stanza 3 not as disjunctive but as conjunctive, not as
"either-or" but as "both-and." For as Eckhart affirms, like St. Bonaventura quoted above, "it must be realized that the word, the *Logos*
or idea of things, is in the things, and indeed wholly in each one
of them, in such a way that it is nevertheless wholly outside each,
wholly within and wholly without." Writing elsewhere on this
same theme, Eckhart tells us that "God is creating this whole world
fully and completely in this Now" and that "God is in all things,

but . . . God is nowhere so properly as in the soul . . . in the innermost of the soul . . . The Father begets His Son in the innermost of the soul, and begets you with His only-begotten Son as not less than Him . . . For St. John says: 'Ye are sons of God.' " [22] "My Spirit" presents poetically, vividly, and concretely the experience behind these words. In and through the Soul or Spirit of man, God creates the whole world, for in *my Spirit* God begets His creative Son, who makes or "begets" all things in an eternal process whereby one's full and true nature is realized. "In my Soul," a Thought begot or was every object. Stanza 4, especially lines 57–58 and 65–68, develops the combined Platonism-Aristotelianism reflected in the idea of the Logos being wholly within and wholly without. And then in the ecstatic, appositive fifth stanza, Traherne properly and precisely concludes that in *my Spirit,* "without Hyperbole, The Son and friend of God we see." As well as its sense of a righteous person who enjoys God's special favor, a meaning associated with James 2:23, "friend" may convey its etymological meanings of "lover" and "free one" (OED), thus echoing the imperative "get free" of "The Preparative" and looking forward to the redeemed "Friend" and "Son" of the final couplet in the poem appropriately entitled "Love."

Traherne's analysis in stanzas 1–4, in the past tense, has led to insight into, among other things, the infinite nature of Spirit in childhood experience: "My Soul a Spirit infinit!" Traherne exclaims in the conclusive fifth stanza, which makes an almost unnoticed shift from the past tense of its line 75 to the present tense of its subsequent lines. After the climax of stanza 5, the divine nature of "childhood's" Spirit is developed mainly by paradox and negation in stanza 6, and then, as prepared for by the tense shift in stanza 5, Traherne turns in the highly ecstatic, appositive, symbolic seventh stanza to his own present state and to fallen man's condition. Roughly speaking, stanza 6 expands the first half of stanza 5, and stanza 7 the second half of stanza 5. In particular, stanza 6 develops the infinite nature of Spirit (both "infinit" and "Infinitie" are used in this stanza) by describing how it proceeded from within "and . . . did evry Way Dilate it self" and by twice denying, as previously the poem affirmed, that *my Spirit* was a sphere (lines 94, 101). Because the mystical experience itself is paradoxical, as surely the experience of Infinity is, Traherne's thought and mode of expression is fundamentally and organically paradoxical; because the whole truth, so contemplatives have held, can be hinted at only by both affirmation and denial Traherne must by paradox travel both the *via positiva* and the *via negativa*. To affirm, as stanza 5 does, that *my Spirit* is "A Strange Mysterious Sphere!" is surely to praise and glorify Spirit, but lest the image of the sphere imply or be taken to imply finite bounds and final definition Traherne must in stanza 6 develop the idea of *my Spirit's* infinite nature and must emphatically also assert that "Twas not a Sphere." The *Logos* or Idea — Spirit or Thought — shines in finite created things, yet is not enclosed or comprehended by them.

Stanza 7 is not merely repetitious of stanza 5 because each appositive term contributes additional meaning rather than being merely synonymously repetitious and especially because lines 103–117 of the last stanza are wholly in the present tense. The shift in tense is evidence that in "My Spirit" Traherne is writing not only of a past, lost, actual and symbolic, and "recoverable" innocent childhood but also of an already recovered, presently enjoyed Felicity. He is presenting an achieved-voice description and celebration of this "Wondrous Self," this "Sphere of Light," an account, in Margoliouth's words, of "the mature man's mystical inner experience" (II, 349). Like "The Preparative," however, "My Spirit" concludes (lines 117–119) with assumed-voice advice, though, unlike "The Preparative," Traherne here seems to be speaking *to* rather than *for* fallen man. Another way of putting this is to say that in the poem's description of childhood's and the redeemed man's creative, spiritual Self and activity Traherne has all along had in mind instruction in Felicity for fallen man.

I believe we may with some justice conclude that Traherne's form and style throughout this poem seem exactly adapted to, suitable for, indeed organically at one with his complex content. Because of the discursive, dichotomous nature of ordinary language and thought and the ineffability of nondual ultimate Reality, attempts to describe that finally ineffable Reality are perhaps best managed and effected through poetic language which is both symbolic and literal, suggestive and precise, repetitive and allusive, paradoxical, and appositive.

We have seen in Chapter One especially that the contemplatives are in agreement about the essential spiritual unity of God and man. In the preceding discussion we have noted some of Traherne's careful efforts to describe, to take one example, the infinite nature of *my Spirit,* infinity being of course one of the traditional attributes ascribed to God. Among Philip's many ruinous changes in his version of "My Spirit" let us observe one particular kind from each of the last three conclusive stanzas:

Thomas:	My Soul a Spirit infinit!	71
Philip:	My Soul a Spirit wide and bright	71
Thomas:	And was a Mind	
	Exerted for it saw Infinitie	100
Philip:	For 'twas a Mind	
	Exerted, reaching to Infinity:	100
Thomas:	O Act, O Power infinit;	105
Philip:	O Pow'r and Act, *next Infinit,*	105

Selected and juxaposed against Thomas' lines, Philip's changes need little comment. Notably, Philip leaves unchanged Thomas' "Yet did appear One infinit" (lines 95–96), probably because he took "did appear" as "seemed" rather than in the sense of "was seen as" or "was manifested as." Whereas his gifted brother deftly maintains a delicate balance, Philip apparently will allow only lines which reveal man's Spirit to be similar to or distinguishable from the Divine Spirit, revising those lines which more obviously suggest an ultimate indivisibility.[23]

The autobiographical element is again most apparent in "The Apprehension" (cf. stanza 12 of "The Improvement"). The first line of this very short fragment refers immediately backward to the vision described in "My Spirit," and so this poem cannot be read independently of the preceding poem. Similarly, the first two lines of "Fullnesse," "That Light, that Sight, that Thought, Which in my Soul at first He wrought" (p. 58), also clearly refer backward to "My Spirit," an indication of that poem's very central importance and perhaps another indication that "The Apprehension" was a later insertion. Much of "Fullnesse," a highly appositive and symbolic poem, suggests a present felicity. In its thirty-seven lines all seven major classes of Traherne's symbols in the thirty-seven Dobell poems are represented.

"Nature," "Ease," and "Speed" continue in different terms to explore and develop the significance of childhood, original and redeemed, for man's fallen state, with emphasis on ruinous custom (see "The Instruction," lines 13–16), on Nature's effect on the soul, on negative theology's doctrine of Unknowing, and on the doctrine of the Golden Mean.

> That Custom is a Second Nature, we
> Most Plainly find by Natures Purity
> For Nature teacheth Nothing but the Truth.
>
> ("Nature," p. 60)

These lines imply that "Custom," served by language and intellect, sometimes, perhaps all too frequently, teaches falsehood. In original, pre-intellectual childhood,

My Senses were Informers to my Heart,
The Conduits of his Glory Power and Art.
His Greatness Wisdom Goodness I did see,
His Glorious Lov, and his Eternitie,
Almost as soon as Born: and evry Sence
Was in me like to som Intelligence.
I was by Nature prone and apt to love
All Light and Beauty, both in Heaven above,
And Earth beneath . . .   (p. 60)

The child's disentangled and unclouded senses knew reality directly and immediately. We saw that "My Spirit" repeatedly uses
sphere symbolism, both affirming and denying that *my Spirit* is a
sphere, in order to show that, before custom, convention, and intellect misinform the unfallen Adam that he is a skin-encapsulated
ego in an alien and hostile universe, the image of divinity is himself an unbounded, creative, enlightening Act. "Nature," variously
linked to "My Spirit" and most obviously so in its fifth line's mention of "my Spirit," tries a different metaphor to convey this
idea, an idea that those who still misconceive of themselves as
skin-encapsulated egos will find most difficult to realize, and,
therefore, an idea that requires varied, repeated expression:

A Secret self I had enclosed within,
That was not bounded with my Clothes or Skin,
Or terminated with my Sight, the Sphere
Of which was bounded with the Heavens here:
But that did rather, like the Subtile Light,
Securd from rough and raging Storms by Night,
Break through the Lanthorns sides, and freely ray
Dispersing and Dilating evry Way:
Whose Steddy Beams too Subtile for the Wind,
Are such, that we their Bounds can scarcely find.   (p. 60)

Like God, who rested after creation, the secret self, pneuma,

> did not move, nor one way go, but stood,
> And by Dilating of it self, all Good
> It strove to see, as if twere present there,
> Even while it present stood conversing here:
> And more suggested then I could discern,
> Or ever since by any Means could learn.   (p. 62)

The "untaught," "unknowing" child, looked at the created, natural world as it is and saw "A World of Endless Joys by Nature made" (p. 62). The poem contains these lines in its conclusion:

> The fountain tho not Known,
> Yet that there must be one was plainly shewn.
> Which fountain of Delights must needs be Lov
> As all the Goodness of the things did prov.   (p. 64)

"Ease," following "Nature," begins "How easily doth Nature teach the Soul" (p. 64). Both nature and childhood, the second group of poems shows, are the deity's truthful instructors of, "fathers" to, the man. "Ease" continues the previously introduced themes of the Golden Mean and, in accord with negative theology, of the unknowability of the Godhead by means of intellect. In what seems the voice of a redeemed man's rediscovery and present vision, Traherne reveals

> That all we see is ours, and evry One
> Possessor of the Whole; that evry Man
> Is like a God Incarnat on the Throne,
> Even like the first for whom the World began;

Whom all are taught to honor serv and lov,
Becaus he is Belovd of God unknown;
And therfore is on Earth it self above
All others, that his Wisdom might be shewn.   (p. 66)

"God unknown" may or may not be an allusion to Acts 17, which tells of Paul's preaching before the Court of Areopagus to the Athenians and his remarking upon the famous Athenian altar bearing the inscription "To the Unknown God," and which concludes by noting that Dionysius the Areopagite accompanied Paul when he left Athens. However this may be, it seems quite likely from context, from considering the concluding lines of "Nature," that Traherne has in mind negative theology's doctrine of Unknowing, stemming mainly from Dionysius the pseudo-Areopagite, according to which the Godhead or "fountain" (Traherne's symbol in "Nature") is unknown to the intellect but known to Wisdom or Love. In this sense of a transcendence of ordinary knowledge, C. E. Rolt remarks that "it is even possible that the word 'Unknowing' was . . . a technical term of the Mysteries or of later Greek Philosophy, and that this is the real explanation and interpretation of the inscription on the Athenian altar: 'To the Unknown God.'"[24] Even though Paul clearly did not take the inscription in this sense, that he himself may nevertheless have to some extent shared the doctrine of Unknowing is sufficiently suggested by his own views on knowledge and love: "though I have *the gift of* prophecy, and understand all mysteries, and all knowledge; and though I have all faith, so that I could remove mountains, and have not charity, I am nothing" (I Cor. 13:2). "Knowledge puffeth up, but charity edifieth. And if any man think that he knoweth any thing, he knoweth nothing yet as he ought to know. But if any man love God, the same is known of him" (I Cor. 8:1-3).

Five. Redemption: "The Designe" to "Goodnesse"

A Miste involvs the Ey,
While in the Middle it doth lie;
And till the Ends of Things are seen,
The Way's uncertain that doth stand between.
                                    "The Demonstration"

What hinders then, but we in heav'n may be
Even here on Earth did we but rightly see?
                                    "Thoughts IV"

THE VARIOUS ALLUSIONS TO MAN's fallen state in the poems following "The Preparative" culminate in the last two stanzas of "Speed," which, spoken in Traherne's assumed voice, refer explicitly to the loss of childhood vision. "The Apprehension," which follows "My Spirit" and is palpably meaningless if read separately, not only indicates that, as Margoliouth observes, "the 'Apprehension' is intellectual and serves its purpose at times when the vision is absent" (II, 351) from the Eye of the redeemed adult, but also suggests that the intellect in such a man is itself redeemed and may thus serve to enlighten other men. After a dedication to Truth ("The Designe") and a celebration of the body and the world ("The Person," "The Estate," and "The Enquirie"), the redeemed intellect is to do just that in "The Circulation" to "Another." In the remaining poems, "Love" leads to "Thoughts" (that is, redeemed imaginative vision) and to "Bliss" and, through the recapitulative "Desire," culminates in "Goodnesse." Understanding the following division and emphasis to be somewhat of an oversimplification for the sake of analysis, we may say that the three poems from "The Person" to "The Enquirie" mainly have to do with the Body and World, the six poems from "The Circulation" to "Another" with the Intellect, and the nine poems from "Love" to "Goodnesse" with the Spirit.

Marking a new beginning, the first stanza of "The Designe" clearly alludes to the Creation Myth in Genesis 1. This allusion and the many references to or symbols for Christ in later poems, along with much else, make it again evident that Traherne's basic model throughout the Folio remains the eternally, constantly operative biblical pattern of the Creation, Fall, Redemption. Like many other Traherne poems, "The Designe" opens very finely: "When first Eternity Stoopd down to Nought" (p. 70). Traherne then develops this poem largely through King symbolism and the imagery of marriage and love. Truth, the Creation, is female, the Daughter of Eternity and, as such, she is

> the Great Queen
> of Bliss, between
> Whom and the Soul, no one Pretender ought
> Thrust in, to Captivat a Thought.   (p. 72)

The pretender is the usurping ego, and, as later lines show, "evry Man" is or ought to be a King, the lover and husband united to the Truth, the Queen of Bliss. According to Traherne, the enlightened man has a sense of reality as erotic; in a very profound sense, the world is his "Bride" (p. 74). Later poems, such as "The Recovery" and "Love," also speak of the redeemed man, in turn, as the Bride of God. That is, Traherne's choice of metaphor and imagery expresses and emphasizes his view that the relationship between the redeemed man and the universe and God is fundamentally one of love.

For various reasons, a question may obtain whether the last two stanzas of "The Designe" refer to original or redeemed "Infancie" or both. In "The Person," however, a poem of the resurrection of the body, Traherne clearly turns to the adult and his redemption, to the meaning of recovered childhood, the primary concern of the remaining poems in the Dobell Folio. The first stanza of "The Person" continues the King symbolism of the preceding poem:

> Ye Sacred Lims,
> A richer Blazon I will lay
> On you, then first I found:
> That like Celestial Kings,
> Ye might with Ornaments of Joy
> Be always Crownd.

> A Deep Vermilion on a Red,
>   On that a Scarlet I will lay,
>   With Gold Ile Crown your Head,
>   Which like the Sun shall Ray.
>   With Robes of Glory and Delight
>   Ile make you Bright.
> Mistake me not, I do not mean to bring
>   New Robes, but to Display the Thing:
> Nor Paint, nor Cloath, nor Crown, nor add a Ray,
> But Glorify by taking all away.   (p. 74)

The first three lines mark a new beginning for the individual by
appropriately echoing the opening lines of "The Salutation,"

> These little Limmes,
>   These Eys and Hands which here I find.   (p. 4)

The stanza's last lines, *seeming* to contradict the preceding lines
because of the playful and witty poetic shift from King and Sun
symbolism to literal language, refer to the purgation of ego, of all
those worldly trappings acquired after early childhood in the
process of growing up, in the Fall.

"The Person" testifies that Traherne consciously parodied or
exploited the blazon convention. Similarly, *Meditations on the Six
Days of the Creation* presents a parodied Petrarchan and Elizabethan catalog of the beauties of the human face, with plainly
biblical overtones and symbolism: "But the Face! O the Wonders
of thy Work, O Lord, in that! . . . The Lips are as Cherries, and
the Cheeks Gardens of Lilies and Roses: The Eyes, like Stars,
are the Fountains of Light, or Sight, which is superior to Splendor:
The Mouth is the Portal of Life and Death, as well as Breath, and
the Gate of Wisdom, without adorn'd with Smiles, and beautified

with Graces: The Teeth within are as a Port-Cullis of Pearl, and the Tongue a Workmanship of infinite Wonder" (p. 77). As Herbert did, Traherne here and in "The Person" transforms a secular convention to his own divine ends. For him, there is indeed a Garden, and more, in the human face, though not in Thomas Campion's sense. The blazon convention too extensively permeates Elizabethan poetry for us to designate, in conjunction with The Song of Solomon, any single poem or even any particular sonnet sequence as Traherne's "model." Furthermore, though several Traherne poems have fourteen-line stanzas, his extant work contains no sonnet.

"The Person," "The Estate," and "The Enquirie" celebrate not fallen man's fabricated, illusional world but God's created works, which include the natural world and especially man's sacred body. Continuing the theme of "The Designe," "The Person" exclaims "Let Veritie Be thy Delight," and its concluding catalog affirms that

> Thy Gifts O God alone Ile prize,
>   My Tongue, my Eys,
> My cheeks, my Lips, my Ears, my Hands, my Feet,
>   Their Harmony is far more Sweet;
> Their Beauty true. And these in all my Ways
> Shall Themes becom, and Organs of thy Praise.   (p. 78)

In "The Estate," we should note, both this catalog of bodily members and the above musical metaphors are returned to and developed, "Themes" and "Organs" being of course here wittily played upon. Again and again, we find that the Dobell Folio poems are interrelated not only by theme but also by key words, metaphors, images, and symbols, often by subtly extended metaphor and plurisignificant words:

We plough the very Skies, as well
  To trie thy Joys upon:
And evry Member ought to be
  A Tongue, to Sing to Thee.
There's not an Ey thats framd by Thee,
  But ought thy Life and Lov, to see.
Nor is there, Lord, upon mine Head an Ear,
But that the Musick of thy Works should hear.
Each Toe, each Finger framed by thy Skill,
      Ought Oyntments to Distill.
  Ambrosia, Nectar, Wine should flow
      From evry Joynt I owe,
Or Things more Rich; while all mine Inward Powers
Are Blessed, Joyfull, and Eternal Bowers.

  They ought, my God, to be the Pipes,
    And Conduits of thy Prais.
  Mens Bodies were not made for Stripes,
    Nor any thing but Joys.
  They were not made to be alone:
  But made to be the very Throne
Of Blessedness, to be like Suns, whose Raies,
Dispersed, Scatter many thousand Ways.
They Drink in Nectars, and Disburs again
      In Purer Beams, those Streams,
    Those Nectars which are causd by Joys.
      And as the spacious Main
Doth all the Rivers, which it Drinks, return,
Thy Love receivd doth make the Soul to burn.   (p. 80)

"Pipes" and "Conduits" carry both their musical sense, organ
pipes or wind instruments blown by the mouth, and the sense of

conveyors and containers of liquid (conduits also meaning fountains) consistent with the stanzas' imagery of water, wine, and other liquids. Because Philip changed stanza 2 disastrously and omitted stanza 3 entirely, the musical metaphors and Fountain and Sun symbolism are substantially reduced in F. Vital connections within "The Estate" and between this poem and other poems throughout the Folio are destroyed by Philip's editing. For example, Thomas' "Wine should flow From evry Joynt," spoken for fallen man, establishes an allusive bridge between the wine symbolism, so fundamentally Christian, of "Wonder," concerned with original childhood, and of "Goodnesse," concerned with the redeemed adult. Philip omitted "Wine" from "The Estate" and, of course, omitted "Goodnesse" altogether. Not only the wine symbolism but also images of drinking and eating become centrally important and increasingly frequent in this last group of poems.

Most notably in its first and last stanzas, "The Estate," in its own distinctive way, reasserts the intimate relationship of subject and object, inner and outer works, and soul and body. The air, for example, is not only to sustain the body but also to please the soul. We are to become conscious that every breath we take and give up is a joyful affirmation and praise of divinity, of pneuma. Philip's changing of "The Souls of Men" to "Our Earthly part," as indeed his version of the entire last stanza, is another precise indication of the widespread inferiority of his readings. Considering the poem's earlier use of alchemical imagery and Traherne's practice of simultaneously employing literal and symbolic meanings, Thomas' last stanza, symbolically read, also tells us that the Sun of righteousness, which is Christ, "the last Adam . . . a quickening spirit," purges, transmutes, refines the first Adam, who "is of the earth earthy" (I Cor. 15:45, 47), into noble metal and precious jewels:

> My Palate ought to be a Stone
> As Earth, the Spacious Seas
> Are ours; the Stars all Gems excell.
> The Air was made to pleas
> The Souls of Men: Devouring fire
> Doth feed and Quicken Mans Desire.
> The Sun it self doth in its Glory Shine,
> And Gold and Silver out of very Mire,
> And Pearls and Rubies out of Earth refine,
> While Herbs and Flowers aspire
> To touch and make our feet Divine.
> How Glorious is Mans Fate
> The Laws of God, the Works he did Create,
> His Ancient Ways, are His, and my Estate.   (p. 82)

Traherne here points to what was indicated by preceding poems in the sequence and will become still more fully and variously developed in subsequent poems: the redeemed man's estate, his substance, is no less than all God's laws, works, ways. To the enlightened man, the universe becomes not just his Bride but his Body; so-called external objects are informers of the body or are the "outer" limits of the Man–World unity, "For Outward Joys and Pleasures Are even the Things for which my Lims are Treasures" (p. 78). As we read in the *Centuries,* "You never Enjoy the World aright, till the Sea it self floweth in your Veins, till you are Clothed with the Heavens, and Crowned with the Stars: and Perceiv your self to be the Sole Heir of the whole World: and more then so, becaus Men are in it who are evry one Sole Heirs, as well as you" (I, 29).

Men of such vision may "Sing becaus the Earth for them doth Shine"; and because such vision includes synesthetic perception and the apprehension of immanent divinity, they may "taste even living Nectar in the Seas" (p. 82).[1] To redeemed men and "Holy Angels," all perception is a form of tasting and eating, spiritual nourishment. Developing many of the images and symbols of preceding poems, "The Enquirie," in its sensuously and symbolically rich stanzas, which may call to mind some of Milton's descriptions of the Garden, presents a vision of recovered Eden, where seeing and feeding are one, and God's works are joy-giving fruits:

> Even Holy Angels may com down
> To walk on Earth, and see Delights,
> That feed and pleas, even here, their Appetites.
>   Our Joys may make a Crown
> For them. And in his Tabernacle Men may be
> Like Palmes we mingled with the Cherubs see.

> Mens Sences are indeed the Gems,
> Their Praises the most Sweet Perfumes,
> Their Eys the Thrones, their Hearts the Heavnly Rooms,
>   Their Souls the Diadems,
> Their Tongues the Organs which they lov to hear,
> Their Cheeks and faces like to theirs appear.

> The Wonders which our God hath done,
> The Glories of his Attributes,
> Like dangling Apples or like Golden Fruits,
>   Angelick Joys become.
> His Wisdom Shines, on Earth his Lov doth flow,
> Like Myrrh or Incense even here below.

> And shall not we such Joys possess,
> Which God for Man did chiefly make?

The Angels hav them only for our sake!
   And yet they all confess
His Glory here on Earth to be Divine,
And that his GODHEAD in his Works doth shine.   (p. 84)

The six poems from "The Circulation" to "Another," poems of
the redeemed intellect, are reasoning, argumentative "philosophical" poems. As the preceding three poems explicitly celebrated
primarily the human body and the natural world, these poems
implicitly celebrate the human mind in its undeluded and resurrected state. For in that state it can help lead man toward what
the child has by "Intuition" and what the saint has by "the Highest Reason" (*C* III 2), for which kind of Reason, Love and Imagination are almost equivalent terms.[2] While realizing its own
limitations, realizing that the Godhead "wilt for evermore Exceed
the End Of all that Creatures Wit can comprehend" ("Amendment," p. 155), the redeemed mind can attempt to demonstrate
intellectually that

> The Highest Things are Easiest to be shewn,
> And only capable of being *Known,*
>   A Miste involvs the Ey,
>   While in the Middle it doth lie;
>   And till the Ends of Things are seen,
> The Way's uncertain that doth stand between.   (p. 156)

These lines from "The Demonstration," which allude to the whole
basic archetypal pattern of the Fortunate Fall, assert that the
cloudy knowledge of the middle fallen state is ultimately but illusion; only when the cycle is completed does the redeemed Eye,
seeing all things in their essence, have certain, self-evident, and
real knowledge.

The poems from "The Circulation" to "Another" present the doctrine of Circulation, which, though it has received some critical comment,[3] has never been discussed in terms of its close vital relation to the doctrine of the Golden Mean, to the Godhead, and to Traherne's theory of perception or imaginative vision. Understanding Traherne's theory of perception, which underlies the entire Redemption group of poems, is a valuable key for more fully appreciating all of Traherne's poetry.

Subtly exploiting the literal and symbolic meanings of several major images and cataloging apt and cogent examples, Traherne contends in "The Circulation" that

> All Things to Circulations owe
> Themselvs; by which alone
> They do exist.   (p. 153)

All things are empty, impotent, as nothing, unless God fills them. "All things do first receiv, that giv" (p. 154). Traherne indeed has a profound sense of humility and of his total dependence on the Eternal Source:

> No Prais can we return again,
> No Glory in our selvs possess,
> But what derived from without we gain,
> From all the Mysteries of Blessedness.   (p. 152)

These lines alone should indicate that Traherne was no subjective idealist nor egotist. In accord with Christian doctrine, only God is described as wholly self-sufficient, and as

> the Primitive Eternal Spring
> The Endless Ocean of each Glorious Thing.   (p. 154)

As Traherne, quoting Quarles, wrote in a notebook (Bodleian MS. Lat. misc. f. 45):

> What e're I have from God alone I have
> and Hee takes pleasure in the gifts he gave.[4] (p. 204)

However, by Traherne's literal and symbolic use of key images, the extraordinary paradox of God's need for man, overtly developed later, is anticipated in "The Circulation":

> No Tenant can rais Corn, or pay his Rent,
>   Nor can even hav a Lord,
>   That has no Land. No spring can vent,
>   No vessel any Wine afford
> Wherein no Liquor's put . . .

> Flame that ejects its Golden Beams,
>   Sups up the Grosser Air;
> To Seas, that pour out their Streams
>   In Springs, those Streams repair;
>   Receivd Ideas make even Dreams.
> No Fancy painteth foule or fair
> But by the Ministry of Inward Light,
> That in the Spirits Cherisheth its Sight.
> The Moon returneth Light, and som men say
>   The very Sun no Ray
>   Nor Influence could hav, did it
>   No forrein Aids, no food admit,
> The Earth no Exhalations would afford,
> Were not its Spirits by the Sun restord.   (p. 154)

For the basic idea of these lines Traherne could have drawn upon numerous sources from Plato's *Timaeus* to Milton's *Paradise*

Lost, V, 414–433 and 470–485. The eating and food metaphors signify that for Traherne the physical-spiritual world is to be regarded as a constant and universal feast. All things in the universe are not isolated fragments but interdependent parts of the whole, sustaining one another. Traherne's primary intention in this poem, however, is to show that man, God's "Vessel," like the natural world, requires filling, receiving, if he is to be spiritually as well as physically nourished. To this end, such terms as springs, seas, and sun function in the literal sense. But because these images, to say nothing of the suggestive "Corn" and "Wine," have previously been charged with multiple symbolic meanings, connoting pneuma, God, and Godhead, the subsequently developed theme of God's need for man is here implicit. Traherne's twofold, reflexive use of recurrent central images is surely remarkable: reading him carefully is often like watching his metaphors and symbols grow and expand in meaning right before one's eyes.

When man, the vessel, is filled by "The Endless Ocean," he returns, "Amendment" continues, the gifts to the Source because God's works are more pleasing to Him after they have been viewed, received and enhanced — activated — by man than they are in themselves as dead material things. All things flow from God and return to Him with increased value for having been received by man — well received, that is. For man's viewing, perception, reception, "The Demonstration" shows, must be of a special kind. If a man does not see a universe in a grain of sand, he sees nothing: the conventional, egotistical mode of perception, which sees the finite only as bounded and finished, is a way of not seeing, that is, of limiting, reducing, excluding vision. Because humankind cannot stand too much reality, such narrowed vision may itself serve a useful and necessary purpose. But truly "normal" vision is imaginative or divine vision, seeing with the Eye of God, or, as we noted in our discussion of "My Spirit," seeing with the heart or Spirit through the eyes. By "the Highest Reason," by contemplative or imaginative vision, when Christ in us sees, God's infinite gifts are infinitely regarded, loved, returned. It is as we read in "Dumnesse," "To see, love, Covet, hav, Enjoy and Prais, in one" (p. 42; note how Traherne's meaning necessitates an appositive style). The idea of return and gratitude to God, implicit and touched upon in earlier poems, is explicitly more fully developed in the Redemption poems. And that all things *are* circulatory both signalizes and symbolizes the perfection of God's created world as it is.

As evidenced by "The Circulation" and "Another," Traherne shares the traditional view that man and his love are as nothing compared to God and his infinite Love. Yet Traherne paradoxically, mystically, goes beyond this view in the second half of "The Demonstration" and in "The Anticipation" to affirm and elaborate overtly the idea of the Godhead's need for man:

> The GODHEAD cannot prize
> The Sun at all, nor yet the Skies,
> Or Air, or Earth, or Trees, or Seas,
> Or Stars, unless the Soul of Man they pleas.

In his creatures, the Godhead "sees, and feels, and Smels, and Lives" ("The Demonstration," pp. 158, 159). "From Everlasting he these Joys did Need" ("The Anticipation," p. 160). Such a position is much more mystical than devotional or meditational. "You are," Eckhart paradoxically asserts, "a thousand times more necessary to him than he is to you." [5]

"The Demonstration," particularly the last stanza, also clearly introduces the almost incredible paradox that the Godhead, the No-thing, is all in all. "Of him, and by him, and in him are all

things," St. Augustine writes, in close paraphrase of Romans
11:36.[6] "The Anticipation," continuing this biblical and Augustinian theme (and even employing in its first stanza the final rime of
the preceding poem), expands this profound and overwhelming
idea that God is indeed the fountain, means, and end; the All.

> My Contemplation Dazles in the End
> Of all I comprehend.
> And soars abov all Heights,
> Diving into the Depths of all Delights.   (p. 159)

Having seized contemplatively, imaginatively, by means of God's
grace, the ultimate truth of God's being all in all, Traherne admirably attempts in "The Anticipation" to make it intellectually,
philosophically, and poetically available to us.

"The Recovery" and "Another" concern, as Margoliouth notes
(II, 391–392), God's recovering his gifts to man:

> Our Blessedness to see
> Is even to the Deitie
> A Beatifick Vision!
>
> ("The Recovery," p. 163)

These Poems thus advise against that which characterizes and
distinguishes the fallen man: hatred of or indifference to God's
works, ways, and love. "Tis Death my Soul to be Indifferent"
("Another," p. 166). Only when his works, ways, and love are
well-received, that is, when childlike vision is recovered, does
God fully realize "his Whole Felicitie." Yet, in going a step
further, Traherne reveals another vital difference between the
child and the enlightened man. Although the child's seeing and
enjoying is itself a kind of unconscious praise, only a redeemed

or at least "recovering" adult can consciously feel, know, and offer "Gratitude, Thanksgiving, Prais."[7] What God most desires and what most delights him is "One Voluntary Act of Love." Thus, echoing yet extending the last stanza of "The Preparative," "The Recovery" concludes:

> Tis not alone a Lively Sence
> A clear and Quick Intelligence
> A free, Profound, and full Esteem:
> Tho these Elixars all and Ends to seem
> But Gratitude, Thanksgiving, Prais,
> A Heart returnd for all these Joys,
>   These are the Things admird,
>   These are the Things by Him desird.
> These are the Nectar and the Quintessence
> The Cream and Flower that most affect his Sence.
>
> The voluntary Act wherby
> These are repaid, is in his Ey
> More Precious then the very Skie.
> All Gold and Silver is but Empty Dross
> Rubies and Saphires are but Loss
> The very Sun and Stars and Seas
>   Far less his Spirit pleas.
> One Voluntary Act of Love
> Far more Delightfull to his Soul doth prove
> And is abov all these as far as Love.   (p. 165)

The assumed voice, expressed largely by first person plural pronouns, of "The Recovery" and especially "Another" appears more didactic and hortatory than it usually does in the Folio, more adopted than natural, more like the assumed voice in "The Instruction" than in, for example, stanza 4 of "The Approach" or the last two lines of "The Preparative." One can readily imagine the speaker in the role of minister or preacher, deliberately saying "we" and "my soul" instead of "you" and "your soul" to his congregation. Indeed, the second half of "Another," after addressing "my Soul" in line 17 (see also line 2), shifts from the poem's earlier use of first person to the second person "Thou," "Thee," and "thy." A question therefore obtains whether the second person pronouns refer to someone other than the speaker or whether, as is more likely, the speaker in an assumed voice is throughout the second part of "Another" pronominally addressing "my Soul" as representative of the soul of every man. In any case, the redeemed man, it should be observed, stands in a difficult position, faced with a curious dilemma: he must not appear presumptuous about salvation, yet he must not utter less than the truth. The possibility of insufficient humility on the one hand and dishonesty on the other confronts such a man. Traherne, we gather from the "Select Meditations," was aware of this problem.[8] Sometimes, then, the assumed voice may be a deliberate and proper assumption of humility and a conscious self-reminder that in the redeemed man "I live; yet not I, but Christ liveth in me" (Gal. 2:20). This is the sense in which the "I" functions in "Love," the poem which immediately follows "Another" and which clearly concerns a redeemed present Felicity.

Although there is a dramatic shift in poetic mode between the reasoning poems from "The Circulation" to "Another" and the several highly ecstatic poems from "Love" to "Goodnesse," all these poems remain interrelated, harmonious parts of one sequential whole. This is in part accomplished by the "Thoughts" poems. But there is more. In the last stanza of "The Recovery," for example, Traherne apparently deliberately altered the poem's couplet rhyme scheme in order to repeat the word Love for the fourth and fifth time in the poem. And he begins "Another," "He seeks for ours as we do seek for his" (p. 165), the implied noun being Love. Love explicitly appears twelve times in this poem's eleven stanzas, Goodness appears five times, and both are frequently referred to pronominally. This is to say that Traherne is carefully preparing his reader for the very ecstatic and appositive "Love" and indeed for all the last nine poems from "Love" to "Goodnesse." Among the most frequently recurring words in the preceding philosophical poems especially and the whole Folio generally (excluding function words, of course) are Love, Goodness, Bliss (and the related Felicity, Joy, Pleasure), Desire (or Want) and Thoughts. Love, the second most frequent word in the Folio, occurs at least seventy-two times and the other words each occur roughly half as many times — that is, as often as many of Traherne's major symbols. (Given Traherne's primary pneuma-revealing intention, Soul is inevitably and appropriately the most frequent word.) Because the words Love, Goodness, Bliss, Desire, and Thoughts "sum up" the poems as well as any five words can and because they are the titles of the last poems, all of these repetitions are functional, directional, and unifying. Traherne no doubt felt the need to prepare his reader carefully for these last poems, for they are his most symbolic and intensely ecstatic and appositive. They are expressive of Spirit or the Total Man ("Sence," "Mind," "Brest," "Intelligence," "Spirit" — "The Preparative" appositively puts it), as the poems from "The Circulation" to "Another" may be said to be expressive of the redeemed intellect.

The primary symbolism of the six poems preceding "Love" is that of the Fountain group; a secondary symbolism, particularly in "The Recovery" and "Another," is that of the King class. In "Love" these symbols are by apposition "united":

> Lo, now I see there's such a King,
> The fountain Head of evry Thing!   (p. 168)

In other words, in addition to deliberate, functional repetition, Traherne prepares his reader by his appositive mode, by his juxtaposition, patterning, combination, and fusion of symbols. If all of this careful preparation is observed and felt, if, that is, the reader takes "Love," in its context, the poem, I contend, will not, cannot, appear "frigid," "ludicrous," insincere, or in "poor taste." [9]

Nor could "Love" be so taken if Traherne's poems were not regarded solemnly. They have more "wit," including the Renaissance meanings of the term, than criticism has yet realized. Let us remember, first, that Traherne was, by his own admission, "a sociable creature, a lover of good company," a "Christian Epicurian," and, by an acquaintance's description, "a man of cheerful and sprightly Temper . . . very affable and pleasant." [10] In the poems, Traherne's "wit" and good humor are, after all, natural and inevitable products and expressions of his Felicity, of the attained state of blessedness which "Love" and other poems show Traherne to have enjoyed. In "Love," wit is most manifest in the dismissal technique which immediately follows the poem's classical allusions:

> Did my Ambition ever Dream
> Of such a Lord, of such a Love! Did I
>   Expect so Sweet a Stream
> As this at any time! Could any Ey
>   Believ it? Why all Power
>   Is used here
> Joys down from Heaven on my Head to shower
> And Jove beyond the Fiction doth appear

Once more in Golden Rain to come.
To Danae's Pleasing Fruitfull Womb.

His Ganimede! His Life! His Joy!
Or he comes down to me, or takes me up
    That I might be his Boy,
And fill, and taste, and give, and Drink the Cup.
    But these (tho great) are all
        Too short and small,
Too Weak and feeble Pictures to Express
The true Mysterious Depths of Blessedness.
    I am his Image, and his Friend.
His Son, Bride, Glory, Temple, End.   (p. 168)

This dismissal of the various images, "Pictures," as inadequate is apt and metaphysically sound because the ultimate vision, "The true Mysterious Depths of Blessedness," is ineffable. And in employing this technique in a poem entitled "Love" which follows "poems of the redeemed intellect," Traherne is being quite precise in that, as mysticism generally holds, it is not by the rational intellect but by love that God is known. Moreover, Traherne subtly and wittily employs appropriate classical allusion, rare in his poetry, just prior to dismissal. The implication is that the specifically Christian symbols of the concluding couplet, symbols which resonate with preceding stanzas of "Love" and with the other poems in the Folio, are superior to the pagan imagery for conveying his meaning. One also sees playfulness in ending the poem with *End* — a repeated word, moreover, of exceeding importance in the previous philosophical poems. That this couplet comes after the assertion of the inadequacy of language seems to confirm, furthermore, that Traherne used his bare catalogs and his appositive technique, as I have suggested, to strike directly at the final and highest truths by a series of shots, as it were, here by a series of pneuma-revealing symbols. When a contemplative chooses to communicate his vision in language, he can, I think, make no wiser decision than to employ symbols enriched by a great tradition and by his own unique reflexive and appositive use of them.[11]

In the interrelatedness of the images and symbols, in the extended metaphors, and the wit of the dismissal technique, a technique similar to Donne's well-known reversal strategy, "Love" assumes a place among other "metaphysical" poems. Yet we will better appreciate this poem, especially the first stanza with its fourteen appositive vocatives, by seeing that Traherne is not only a part of a tradition of wit and complexity but also heir to an Elizabethan and Jonsonian tradition of lyric intensity. Traherne is a singer. It is a simple fact, one that can easily be verified, that his poems are better in being read aloud. The first stanza of "Love," as indeed the whole poem, seems radically transformed for the better when read aloud by an accomplished reader. Traherne's catalogs and appositions, which especially require skilled reading, are capable of establishing by means of their rhythms alone strong and varied emotional effects. It is of no little significance that Traherne's poetry *sounds* like poetry. Living at a time when reading aloud was far more customary than it is today, Traherne, one can readily imagine, may have written his poems first to be read to a circle of friends, perhaps in Sir Orlando Bridgman's household, and then to be published. Several lines support such a possibility: for example, from "Dumnesse," "This, my Dear friends, this was my Blessed Case." Other lines (such as "My Spirit," lines 47, 67–68, "Thoughts I," line 18, and "Ye hidden Nectars," line 16) seem to require the speaker to point with his finger.

The aural qualities of any body of poems are of course fundamentally related to the poet's craftsmanship. Far from being indifferent to his craft, as some critics have been wont to say,[12] Traherne seems to have been scrupulously attentive to the technical features of his poetry. Other critics have rightly remarked on his skillful use of meter, rhythm, and stanzaic patterns. John Rothwell Slater, for example, points out that in both prose and poetry, Traherne's capitals "are a key to the emphasis and rhythm . . . He undertook to record by his apparently capricious capitals the intonations of the voice, by his colons and semicolons the pause of oral interpretation. He wrote for the ear, and should be read aloud." Allan H. Gilbert comments on Traherne's "careful labor in prose as well as in verse. Whatever the ecstasy of his feeling, his hand is still steady with the polishing tool . . . Such willingness to undertake careful work explains the elaborate stanzas in which he delighted . . . Yet these stanzas, carried sometimes to virtuosity, yield nothing to those of Vaughan in their metrical flow. The ease of the language is the more astonishing because of the thought the verses carry."[13]

It is generally true, my own investigations have shown, that Traherne's stanzaic forms are related to the difficulty of content, and to the degree to which the poem is symbolic, ecstatic, and appositive. With very few exceptions (and excluding the heroic couplet, which is not in any case a stanzaic form), the more difficult, symbolic, ecstatic, or appositive the poem is, the more complex the stanzaic form is. For example, "Ease," given its title, content, theme ("How easily doth Nature teach the Soul," p. 64), and direct mode, is appropriately written in simple iambic pentameter quatrains, rhyming abab. The difficult, symbolic, appositive "My Spirit," Traherne's most comprehensive poem, is, correlatively, written in his most complex stanzaic form: seventeen lines ranging from dimeter to pentameter, with an elaborate scheme of seven rhymes. The poems from "The Salutation" to "The Pre-parative," increasingly more difficult and symbolic, are progressively more complex stanzaically. The poems from "Love" to "Goodnesse" are among the most stanzaically interesting and subtle in themselves and in their possible relationships. For example, the first two "Thoughts" poems are written in twelve-line stanzas with the same rhyme scheme (aabccbddeeff — that is, almost in couplets) but differing line lengths varying from dimeter to pentameter; the middle, ecstatic "Thoughts" poem, "Ye hidden Nectars," consists of ten-line stanzas, each concluded by a heroic couplet; the last two "Thoughts" poems are written in heroic couplets; "Goodnesse" is in twelve-line stanzas, consisting each of six couplets. Thus there is a stanzaic "tying together" or completion and, as the ten-line last stanza of "Goodnesse" may imply, a return to unity and silence. Such examples can be multiplied and many relevant details discussed at length. My point is that all preliminary evidence and the best criticism testify that Traherne is a master craftsman. He appears to have had a considerable respect for poetry, not only for its didactic value as a mode of enlightenment and joyful vision, but also for its aesthetic value as a mode of expression and source of pleasure. The man who took such care as never to repeat a stanzaic form in a second poem in the Dobell Folio nor, with one exception (the "Fourth Day" and "Sixth Day" of *Hexameron*), in his total poetic work indeed must have had a love for his medium as well as for his fellow men.

If we read out of context "Thoughts I," stanzas 6–7, or certain other passages in his work, we might mistakenly assume that Traherne simply falls into the old body-soul dualism, with all its usual implications of the body as grossly inferior. But when we closely read the "Thoughts" poems against one another and in the sequence it becomes clear that the very inclusive term thoughts sometimes refers to sensuous perceptions, especially perceptions by the redeemed man's resurrected body. Although there is development in the "Thoughts" poems and although they are stanzaically and imagistically interrelated and continuous, thoughts are not discriminated into kinds to be separately treated in each poem. Very much like Whitman's "Eidólons," the word thoughts includes not only percepts, but also concepts, prayers, ideals, practical ideas, images, memories, feelings, and emotions: appropriately so, since Traherne's interest lies in the redemption of the whole man. We must therefore not restrict "thought" to its usual meaning of logical, discursive, conceptualizing thinking but rather understand it primarily as the activity of the Highest Reason, as imaginative, contemplative, noetic activity, which may include yet transcends all other activities. We come closer to Traherne by changing the Cartesian formula, "I think; therefore I am," arrived at by doubt, to "I imagine; therefore I am" or better "pneuma contemplates; therefore all is," arrived at by joyful affirmation. Whereas the young child's mode of apprehending is intuitive, and the fallen Adam's is primarily ratiocinative, the redeemed Adam's is imaginative or contemplative in this expanded sense, or "angelic," as Milton similarly held. Thus Traherne begins "Thoughts III,"

> Thoughts are the Angels which we send abroad,
> To visit all the parts of Gods Abode. (p. 175)

And comparably he opens "Thoughts IV,"

> Thoughts are the Wings on which the Soul doth flie,
> The Messengers which soar abov the Skie. (p. 179)

The related issues of Traherne's supposed subjectivism and his philosophical or mystical idealism, as well as his theory of perception, all arise most prominently in the "Thoughts" poems, which proceed from and build upon preceding poems, especially the philosophical poems. Any discussion of Traherne's idealism must begin with the firm realization that Traherne, unlike Gnostics and Manicheans, does not regard the body and the physical world as evil but rather lauds, loves, enjoys them. (A question may arise, then, as to how his idealism is to be reconciled with his frequent celebrations of and thanksgivings for the body and the sensuous world throughout the *Meditations on the Six Days of the Creation,* the *Thanksgivings,* and *Centuries,* as well as in the poems.) Next, it must be emphasized that Traherne is neither a subjectivist nor an objectivist. If the term did not already have too many meanings, he might best be called a realist, for he is most in touch with what now is, not living the life of the ego, which feeds upon the dead past or the fancied future. Traherne's "idealism" is actually a profound realism, a thoroughgoing grasp and understanding of the way things actually are:

> What were the Skie,
> What were the Sun, or Stars, did ye not lie
>   In me! and represent them there
>   Where els they never could appear!
> Yea What were Bliss without such Thoughts to me,
> What were my Life, what were the Deitie?
>
> ("Thoughts I," p. 170)

We have seen that in Traherne's view, subject and object, perceiver and percept, are necessary to each other, are inextricably interrelated. Rightly understood, thoughts, the product or result, so to speak, of a conjunctive subject and object or perceiver and physical datum, are the single reality which is life, the deity. A thought, to use Eckhart's terms, is both the "product" and the "producer," the so-called external world and the essential Spirit or creative power which quickens that otherwise dead material world. Looked at one way, Traherne's development of the meaning of thought throughout the Dobell Folio appears to be an attempt to arrive at or formulate a single word that would stand for the various and complex but nevertheless paradoxically single Reality apprehended in mystic experiences. Parmenides had said that "it is the same thing to think and to be." Quoting Parmenides, Plotinus, who contended in his polemic against the Gnostics that the physical world is not to be deplored but rather is full of beauty, elsewhere wrote: "Clearly in The Intelligence, subject and object are one. This identity is more than a close association such as we find in the best of souls because 'it is the same thing to think and to be.' In The Intelligence we no longer have upon one side the object of contemplation and on the other that which contemplates . . . In The Intelligence the two things are one . . . All life is thought." [14] We recall the lines "I was . . . A Naked Simple Pure *Intelligence*" (p. 20) from "The Preparative" and "My Naked Simple Life was I" (p. 50) from "My Spirit," and observe that in "Thoughts III" Traherne writes that

> All Wisdom in a Thought doth Shine,
> By Thoughts alone the Soul is made Divine   (p. 175)

and that a thought "is the only Being that doth live" (p. 176).

Traherne's constant effort is to make the basic tenets of his mystical philosophy clearly and profoundly realized by giving them variously repeated and new expression which will reveal and extend his meaning. In a different way, by focusing on thoughts, Traherne is developing in this last group what is implied about the subject-object relationship throughout the Folio and what is implied in the doctrine of the Golden Mean. The world as God created it, including both creatures and created objects, is excellent and perfect, ineffably so. The material, objective world would be dead, inert, unrealized, if there were no loving spectator to perceive and enjoy it, just as the spectator would be senseless and empty were there no objects to sense: "Life without Objects is a Sensible Emptiness. Objects without Lov are the Delusion of Life" (*C* II 65; see also *C* II 90, 91). To put it a mathematical way, one times zero equals zero; one times one equals One. Which is to say, Thou art That. Thus the idea or thought in the Spirit or heart ("Thoughts I," stanzas 1 and 6, for example) is more precious to God, for it is his objective, material world imaginatively activated or quickened by the enlightened perceiver and returned to him.

> This Sight which is the Glorious End
> Of all his Works, and which doth comprehend
>   Eternity, and Time, and Space,
>   Is far more dear,
>   And far more near
> To him, then all his Glorious Dwelling Place.
>   It is a Spiritual World within.
> A Living World, and nearer far of Kin
>   To God, then that which first he made.
>   While that doth fade
>   This therfore ever shall Endure,
> Within the Soul as more Divine and Pure.
>
> ("Thoughts II," p. 173)

Christ dwelling in man eternally creates the living world out of sheer love, joy, play.

As we have seen, for Traherne, as for the contemplatives generally, all things are in God, and God, who is all Act, is in all things. Our finite minds, our conventionalizing eye and conceptualizing psyche, perceive disordered plurality, but the timeless and spaceless Spirit seizes all things in their unity; in God's mind everything is eternally now. We read in "The Anticipation," for example, that "His Name is Now, his Nature is forever" and "His Essence is all Act" (pp. 160, 162; see also *C* III 62, 65). And in right apprehension, when "My Spirit" also is all Act, when thoughts are "Good,"

> They bear the Image of their father's face,
> And Beautifie even all his Dwelling Place:
> So Nimble and Volatile, unconfind,
> Illimited, to which no Form's assignd,
> So Changeable, Capacious, Easy, free,
> That what it self doth pleas a Thought may be.
> From Nothing to Infinitie it turns,
> Even in a Moment: Now like fire it burns,
> Now's frozen Ice: Now shapes the Glorious Sun,
> Now Darkness in a Moment doth become,
> Now all at once: Now crowded in a sand,
> Now fils the Hemisphere, and sees a land:
> Now on a Suddain's Wider then the Skie,
> And now runs Parile with the Deitie.
>
> ("Thoughts III," p. 176)

For Traherne, eternity is not so much endless time, time piled up on top of time, as it is a no-time or expanded Now-moment: "Eternity is a Mysterious Absence of Times and Ages: an Endless Length of Ages always present, and for ever Perfect" (*C* V 7).

Similarly, as the above poetic passage attests, the world is to be understood as activity, process, rather than as substance. Substances, whether material or ideal, are, like clock time, fictions,

abstract concepts, constructs, if substance be understood as an un-
perceived, unfelt, unimaginable Lockeian substrate or Kantian
Ding an sich. With the Christian contemplatives and Plotinus and
with such later philosophers as Berkeley, F. H. Bradley, and Josiah
Royce, Traherne holds, without denying the existence of an external material world, that the external reality which one thinks
of as an object is in actuality one with oneself. To *Esse est percipi,*
Traherne would add that perceiving, conceiving, imagining, is
being. One is all that one is now seeing, feeling, doing, recollecting,
thinking, contemplating. Thus Traherne insists on seeing that all
things are interrelated and on thoroughly enjoying and esteeming
the world, even the seemingly insignificant grain of sand. We and
the grain come into being, as it were, in the act, activity, of perception. We are the grain of sand; it is us. As the images of
creation and fruitfulness in these last poems underscore, the joy
of perception or even the sensation of pain is a creative or re-
creative act. Accept and affirm it, Traherne would say, and be at
one with it, not divided against it. To deny it, not to give oneself
wholly to it, is, paradoxically, to deny oneself. Not to love is to
die: this is Christ's wisdom. *"Lukewarmness* is Profane" (*CE,* p.
89). There is, in fact, no alternative to an open, thoroughgoing
receptivity, which consequently is creativity; no alternative to
joyous acceptance and affirmation, to wholehearted, zestful sensing,
feeling, thinking; no alternative but half-living, death. We recall
St. Augustine: "And since all those who think of God think of
something living, only they can think of Him without absurdity
who think of Him as life itself." [15] And we remember this couplet
from *Christian Ethicks:*

> Life! Life is all: in its most full extent
> Stretcht out to all things, and with all content.   (p. 218)

All of which is to say not my will, but Thy Will be done.

The more one reads the last poems in the Dobell Folio, these poems of Traherne's idealism or his full and total response to life, the less abstract they appear. We find in Traherne what Eliot has said we find in Donne: "a direct sensuous apprehension of thought, or a recreation of thought into feeling . . . A thought . . . was an experience; it modified his sensibility. When a poet's mind is perfectly equipped for its work, it is constantly amalgamating disparate experience." [16] Doubtlessly, in all ages (not just after the middle of the seventeenth century), the sensibility of most men is dissociated, for dissociated sensibility is but another characteristic of the fallen, unredeemed condition. Whatever the validity of Eliot's theory of the dissociation of sensibility, which he himself later qualified, his quoted remarks do have some pertinence, intended or not, to Traherne. For the state of being about and toward which Traherne writes is an undissociated state, a state in which a man is an integrated, whole human being, a state (to use the traditional terminology) of beatitude or salvation. This state is the central object and end of his writing. Like Milton's Paradise poems and Wordsworth's *The Prelude,* Traherne's Dobell poems can fruitfully be regarded as a quest to reunite feeling and thought. The Grail, the Rose, the Promised Land, is the achievement of "a paradise within," a "feeling intellect," "Imagination," body-mind-soul at its highest pitch. For Traherne, there is finally no separation between thought and feeling, thought and life.

> Ye brisk Divine and Living Things,
> . . . ye are pent within my Brest,
> Yet rove at large from East to West.
>
>   ("Thoughts I," p. 169)

A thought, the interaction of material object and perceiving subject, is in here or out there, as you wish. That is, the third stanza of "My Spirit," the famous "Berkeleian" stanza, is quite exact in presenting alternatives. Or we may say that a thought is neither in nor out, then nor later; it is now and here, eternal and everywhere. Insofar as Traherne's idealism is itself a celebration of life (a recognition of the interrelatedness of subject and object, a realization that subject and object need and "are" each other and that the perfectly created world is eternally re-created every moment) the "Thoughts" series is reconciled with his repeated celebrations of the sensuous world and his recurrent thanksgivings for the body. The world and the body are "thoughts"; that is, without an imaginative subject they cease to be living, just as the subject ceases to be without the world, the body.

In "The Preparative," we read that the nonconceptualizing, newly born child "had the Hony even without the Stings" (p. 20). In "Thoughts III" we read that

> Thoughts are the Things wherin we all confess
> The Quintessence of Sin and Holiness
> Is laid . . .
>   The Hony and the Stings
> Of all that is, are Seated in a Thought.   (pp. 175-176)

By thoughts (of psyche), one falls; by thoughts, in the enlarged sense (of pneuma), one is redeemed. A thought is "such, that it may all or Nothing be."

> The very Best or Worst of Things it is,
> The Basis of all Misery or Bliss.   (pp. 176-177)

How this may be, is revealed in the complex "Desire" (pp. 177-179), a recapitulative and strongly appositive poem, which, with its basic fire and water imagery, its symbolism of the Sun and Fountain groups, is a model of Traherne's reflexive use of language.

This use of language, this characteristic interweaving of clusters of images and symbols drawn primarily from biblical and contemplative literature, leads to a richness that defies exhaustive analysis; but a few examples, from the first four lines of "Desire," may profitably be pointed to, for reflexiveness is itself an essential poetic device for making apparent the full meaning of "Thoughts."

> For giving me Desire,
> An Eager Thirst, a burning Ardent fire,
> A virgin Infant Flame,
> A Love with which into the World I came.
>
> (p. 177)

Not only does "A Love with which into the World I came" remind the reader of "Love" (and the first poems of the whole sequence, "The Salutation" through "The Preparative"), but also, more subtly, "An Eager Thirst" recalls "Ganimede," the cupbearer of "Love," who is to "fill, and taste, and give, and Drink the Cup" (p. 168). "Love" and "Desire," then, resonate with the poem beginning "Ye hidden Nectars, which my God doth drink," an ecstatic, appositive "Thoughts" poem appearing in the center of the poems from "Love" to "Goodnesse." Speaking of thoughts that, through the imagination, give life, allow the Eye to see in a whole and holy manner, Traherne begins the last stanza of "Ye hidden Nectars":

> O what Incredible Delights, What Fires,
> What Appetites, what Joys do ye
> Occasion, what Desires . . .   (p. 175)

Thus, these lines, as also "Enflame the Soul with Love" (p. 173) from "Thoughts II," look forward to "a burning Ardent fire, A virgin Infant Flame" in "Desire." Traherne's quest for union and his metaphysic of the interrelatedness of all things in the universe find brilliant correlative expression in the formal and stylistic devices of an ordered, unified sequence of poems and reflexive and appositive language.

The third stanza of "Desire" has been criticized as trite and re-petitively diffuse.[17] Yet the critic gives no sign of seeing that this "pastoral" stanza is deliberately reflexive and potentially ripe with traditional and appositive symbolic values which Traherne has painstakingly developed throughout the Folio:

> Where are the Silent Streams,
> The Living Waters, and the Glorious Beams,
> The Sweet Reviving Bowers,
> The Shady Groves, the Sweet and Curious Flowers,
> The Springs and Trees, the Heavenly Days,
> The Flowry Meads, the Glorious Rayes,
> The Gold and Silver Towers?
> Alass, all these are poor and Empty Things,
> Trees Waters Days and Shining Beams
> Fruits, Flowers, Bowers, Shady Groves and Springs,
> No Joy will yeeld, no more than Silent Streams.
> These are but Dead Material Toys,
> And cannot make my Heavenly Joys.   (p. 178)

Most impressively, this stanza is not only latently symbolic but also ingeniously literal. The repetition and the last couplet should make it plain that Traherne quite literally means

> Trees Waters Days and Shining Beams
> Fruits, Flowers, Bowers, Shady Groves and Springs.

These "objects" of the Garden here in stanza 3 "are but Dead Material Toys," like "Those little new Invented Things" (p. 171) of "Blisse," a poem in which, however, the antimaterialism is more ethical than ontological. Again, considering context fully is essential to understanding Traherne, for "Blisse," like "Thoughts III," adumbrates that last couplet of stanza 3:

> All Blisse
> Consists in this,
> To do as Adam did:
> And not to know those Superficial Toys
> Which in the Garden once were hid.
>
>   . . . only foolish Men
> Grown mad with Custom on those Toys
> Which more increase their Wants do dote.
>
> (pp. 171–172)

The Garden, God's world, loses its gleam, becomes like man's world of manufactured and avariciously desired things, when mad man with a greedy, conventional eye sees little in nature that is his own.

"Desire" is a summary poem: stanza 1, much like the first group of poems in the Folio, celebrates and gives thanks for God's essential gifts to man at his birth; stanzas 2 and 3, like many lines in the second group, are concerned with the fallen state; stanza 4, like "Love," suggests that by Love, Christ, we are redeemed; and stanza 5 most clearly relates "Desire" to the "Thoughts" poems:

> This Soaring Sacred Thirst,
> Ambassador of Bliss, approached first,
> Making a Place in me,

That made me apt to Prize, and Taste, and See,
     For not the Objects, but the Sence
     Of Things, doth Bliss to Souls dispence,
          And make it Lord like Thee.
Sence, feeling, Taste, Complacency and Sight,
     These are the true and real Joys,
The Living Flowing Inward Melting, Bright
And Heavenly Pleasures; all the rest are Toys:
     All which are founded in Desire,
          As Light in Flame, and Heat in fire.   (p. 179)

With the realization that "not the Objects, but the Sence Of Things, doth Bliss to Souls dispence," the Dobell Folio comes round full circle to "The Preparative" (stanza 6, in particular), the poem which immediately follows Traherne's statement of theme: "I must becom a Child again" (p. 18). "I saw moreover that it did not so much concern us what Objects were before us, as with what Eys we beheld them; with what Affections we esteemed them, and what Apprehensions we had about them. All men see the same Objects, but do not equally understand them . . . All Objects are in God Eternal: which we by perfecting our faculties are made to Enjoy . . . for Life is perfect when it is perfectly Extended to all Objects, and perfectly sees them and perfectly loves them" (*C* III 68). To make the central insight of "Desire" still clearer and to show how characteristic it is of Traherne, we might also consider this parallel and key mystical passage in *Christian Ethicks*:

But if we excite and awaken our Power, we take in the Glory of all objects, we live unto them, we are sensible of them, we delight in them, we transform our souls into Acts of Love and Knowledge, we proceed out of our selves into all

Immensities and Eternities, we render all Things their Due, we reap the Benefit of all, we are Just, and Wise, and Holy, we are Grateful to GOD, and Amiable in being so: We are not divided from, but united to him, in all his Appearances, Thoughts, Counsels, Operations; we adorn our souls with the Beauty of all objects whatsoever, are transformed into the Image of GOD, live in communion with him, nay live in him, and he in us, are made Kings and Priests unto GOD, and his sons forever; There is an exact and pleasant Harmony between us and all the Creatures: We are in a Divine and spiritual Manner made as it were Omnipresent with all Objects (for the Soul is present only by an Act of the understanding) and the Temple of all Eternity does it then becom, when the Kingdom of GOD is seated within it, as the world is in the Eye; while it lives, and feels, and sees, and enjoyes, in every object to which it is extended, its own & its objects Perfection.

(pp. 52–53)

Far from being diffuse and trite, Traherne's poetry is actually economic and rich. In "Desire," both the literal and symbolic uses of key words, Traherne's catalogs and his appositive style or technique, underscore God's full immanence or the world's full being in God. And this twofold poetic mode is an effective way of enabling us to see immediately and profoundly that the Total Man *is* the universe of which he is truly, lovingly, conscious, and that we "live in Him, and He in us." If the Silent Streams, and so on, lie dead and barren, if a man does not ecstatically view them, if he is indifferent to them, then the man himself is in some important sense among the living dead. As suggested earlier, to the enlightened man the universe becomes his body or, let us say more precisely for Traherne, his Body-Soul.[18] Of Body and Soul, Traherne holds not that they are one but that ultimately they are not two; our logical categories, being abstract mental constructs, simply do not finally apply to the concrete and living. Body-Soul and Man-World in opposition would be death; in apposition, Life. In other words, by the sense or by "Thoughts" (the single concrete reality which is the relation or interaction of subject and object), by imaginative vision, by love, by Christ in us, the Wasteland is transformed into the Garden or Heavenly City ("The Sweet Reviving Bowers" or "The Gold and Silver Towers"), the Silent Streams are restored and become the truly "Living Waters" (p. 181) of "Thoughts IV," the literal objects (cumulatively pointed to) acquire symbolic values (appositively presented), are seen, that is, as infinite, as charged with the grandeur of God — are seen not just as our own but as our Self. Redemption lies in seeing the seemingly merely cumulative as actually wholly appositive, wholly interrelated. And this realization is the central point and the main function or purpose of two major features of Traherne's poetry. To see properly the relational or interrelational reality of the world is to see God's objects in God's manner, and such a sight "is a Great Part of the Beatifick Vision" (*C* III 55–60). The final harmony is bestowed, the fallen body and soul are resurrected, polymorphous love is recovered, with the gift of the simple and profound wisdom that "Sence, feeling, Taste, Complacency and Sight . . . are the true and real Joys."

Joy, great, ineffable joy is one of the most distinctive marks of the mystic life, and it characterizes and pervades so much of Traherne's work that one must conclude he knew it deeply and frequently, if not constantly, in his own life. Writing on the mystical joy of the unitive life — the unitive state being "in essence a fulfillment of love; the attainment of a 'heart's desire' " — Evelyn Underhill describes that joy in terms which seem exactly pertinent to Traherne: "That fruition of joy of which Ruysbroeck speaks in majestic phrases, as constituting the interior life of mystic souls immersed in the Absolute — the translation of the Beatific Vision into the terms of a supernal feeling-state — is often realized in the secret experience of those same mystics, as the perennial possession of a childlike gaiety, an inextinguishable gladness of heart." [19] In the mystics generally, love and joy appear as the most prominent attributes of ultimate reality itself. Thus in the *Paradiso*, Dante sees Love smiling (XX, 13); sees, in the doxology of all Paradise, a smile of the universe and ineffable joy (XXVII, 1–7); sees, finally, the Trinity love and smile (XXXIII, 124–126).

The Beatific Vision of Dante's last canto moves from a comprehension of the world unified by Love to a vision of the triune God to a view of the Incarnation. Traherne, I believe, similarly experienced such threefold Vision. That he saw divine Love immanently illuminate the natural, nonhuman world is everywhere apparent throughout his writings, and in the poems reaches a brilliant climax in "Desire." That he knew the vision of the Incarnation, or of Agape as it is sometimes alternately called, is equally apparent, particularly if we rightly understand his pneuma-revealing symbols in his work or properly read such a poem as "Goodnesse." Whether Traherne enjoyed the vision of God has been doubted by some critics, who, without specifying precisely what they mean by the distinction, hold that Traherne believed in communion and not union with God. Although the question, which is more biographical than literary, perhaps cannot be answered with absolute certainty, a careful study of Traherne's work, I believe, strongly suggests he was so blessed. Previous critics did not have the "Select Meditations," but they could have discovered as much from other Traherne writings, for most of his work is of one consistent, developing whole.

Among the most pertinent passages in the "Select Meditations" is this poetic prayer from the Third Century, 58, indicating Traherne's desire for if not actual attainment of union:

> In Silence See the Deity
> The God of Lov
> And ever be
> Within thy Selfe Like Him above
> In union Liv with thy most glorious freind . . .

This poem is followed later in the same Century by an extended discussion of union, which also sheds light on some of the differences between innocent, original childhood and redeemed "childhood." Part of that discussion reads:

> If God hath don for man the Best of all possible Things why then did He not at first make him in the Hypostatical union . . . In the Estate of Innocency that man should personally be united to God was vain and superfluous because there it was no need that God should die but onely be enjoyed, which then might easily and perfectly be don by the Benefit and communion of Lov alone. The union of Lov is the compleatest union, and in it selfe the most Beatifique . . . It was Sin alone that made the Hypostatical union possible. (III, 92)

> The union of Love is so Great an union that the 3 persons in the Trinity are united in it. It is the union of God. And the two natures of our Saviour are united by it . . . But the union of our Soul with God is more sublime [than the union of souls]. He being more us by the force of Love than our very selves. He liveth in us while we contemplat and Admire Him . . . By seeing and Loveing Him we are Transformed into Him become his Similitude

feel his Blessedness, Enjoy his Glory, possess his Treasures and become his own. (III, 93)

Traherne here seems to use the terms union and communion interchangeably, synonymously, as he frequently does in the *Centuries*. Sometimes communion seems to include union, as indeed the first word, as word, includes the second:

> Verily you ought to will these Things so ardently: that GOD Himself should be therfore your Joy because He Willed them. Your Will ought to be United to His in all Places of His Dominion. Were you not Born to hav Communion with Him? And that cannot be without this Heavenly Union. Which when it is what it ought is Divine and Infinit. You are GODS Joy for Willing what he willeth. For He loves to see you Good and Blessed. And will not you lov to see Him Good? Verily if ever you would enjoy God, you must enjoy His Goodness. All His Goodness to all His Hosts in Heaven and Earth. And when you do so, you are the Universal Heir of God and All Things. GOD is yours and the Whole World. You are His, and you are all; Or in all, and with all. (*C* I 53)

Only pneuma can will as God wills and live in union and communion with him, for the psyche is exactly that deluded mode of consciousness which asserts "my will be done." Traherne, we should note, opens the *Centuries* by indicating "the End for which we are Redeemed: A Communion with Him in all His Glory" (I, 5). He knows very well that "In GOD you are Crowned, in GOD you are concerned. In Him you feel, in Him you liv, and mov and hav your Being. in Him you are Blessed" (I, 52). Later in the autobiographical *Third Century* he promises to show his reader "by what Steps and Degrees I proceeded to that Enjoyment of all Eternity which now I possess" (6); "So that it is my Admiration and Joy, that while so many thousand wander in Darkness, I am in the Light, and that while so many Dote upon fals Treasures and Pierce themselves thorow with many Sorrows, I live in Peace, and Enjoy the Delights of God and Heaven" (31); and again, "So that through His Blessing I liv a free and a Kingly Life, as if the World were turned again into Eden, or much more, as it is at this Day" (46). In the *Fourth Century,* Traherne quotes Pico della Mirandola on man, apparently alluding to the Divine Darkness of the pseudo-Areopagite: "And if being content with the lot of no Creatures, he withdraws Himself into the Centre of His own Unitie, he shall be one Spirit with GOD, and Dwell abov all in the Solitary Darkness of his Eternal Father" (77); shortly thereafter (*C* IV 79 ff.) Traherne rearticulates and explains as much in his own words. Finally, of all the many pertinent passages from Traherne, pre-eminently a poet and mystic of joyful love, let this last one from the *Centuries* suffice to suggest that he knew and enjoyed union:

> Were not lov the Darling of GOD, this would be a Rash and a bold Salley. But since it is His Image, and the Lov of GOD, I may almost say the GOD of GOD, becaus His Beloved: all this Happeneth unto Lov. And this Lov is your tru Self when you are in Act what you are in Power. the Great Daemon of the World, the End of all Things. the Desire of Angels and of all Nations. A creature so Glorious, that having seen it, it puts an End to all Curiosity and Swallows up all Admiration. Holy, Wise, and Just towards all Things, Blessed in all Things, the Bride of GOD, Glorious before all, His Offspring and first Born, and so like Him that being described, one would think

it He. I should be afraid to say all this of it, but that I know Him, How He delighteth to hav it magnified. (*C* IV 67)

All of these representative prose passages indicate that Traherne realized much more than the brief impermanent joys which the mystic experiences in the stage of illumination. In the Dobell Folio poems, too, Traherne repeatedly speaks of his Felicity and his Vision as a present, constant possession or state. Remembering that Traherne uses words with the precision expected of a poet and considering the lines in the context of the poems and of Traherne's total work, we can see that these lines from "The Vision," especially as compared to the weakened F version, refer to the abiding Vision of God in the unitive stage:

> To see the *Fountain* is a Blessed Thing.
>   It is to see the King
> Of Glory face to face: But yet the End,
>   The Glorious Wondrous End is more;
> And yet the fountain there we Comprehend,
>   The Spring we there adore.
> For in the End the Fountain best is Shewn,
>   As by Effects the Caus is Known.
>
> From One, to One, in one to see *All Things*
>   To see the King of Kings
> At once in two; to see his Endless Treasures
>   Made all mine own, my self the End
> Of all his Labors! Tis the Life of Pleasures!
>   To see my self His friend!
> Who all things finds conjoynd in Him alone,
>   Sees and Enjoys the Holy one.   (p. 28)

Or from "Silence":

> The Union was so Strait between them two,
> That all was eithers which my Soul could view.

> The World was more in me, then I in it.
> The King of Glory in my Soul did sit.
> And to Himself in me he always gave,
> All that he takes Delight to see me have.   (pp. 48, 50)

These last six lines in context refer primarily to original child-hood, but that estate is, we need not be reminded, a metaphor for the redeemed state. In "Love," a poem which accords remarkably with *C* IV 67 and the "Select Meditations" and the two poems just quoted, Traherne clearly writes of the redeemed state and vision as his present estate. The reader is referred to "Love" in its en-tirety; I quote here only these few lines:

> Did not I covet to behold
> Som Endless Monarch . . .
>> Lo, now I see there's such a King,
>> The fountain Head of evry Thing!

>> I am his Image, and his Friend.
>> His Son, Bride, Glory, Temple, End.   (p. 168)

We should now see these words charged with greater meaning than they ordinarily, on first look, carry. If Traherne did not en-joy union, what English poet did? But, perhaps, the issue, as long as it contains an unanswerable biographical element, is academic. What is important is that no other body of English poetry com-municates a greater sense of Wonder, Joy, and Love, of union or communion with God.[20]

"Love," we have said, leads to "Thoughts" (redeemed imagi-native, contemplative vision) and to "Bliss" and, through the recapitulative "Desire," culminates in "Goodnesse." "Love" follows the poems of the intellect and begins the poems of the Spirit or redeemed Total Man because, for all that man's intellect can do, it is God's freely bestowed gift of love which finally redeems him. "Love" and "Goodnesse" frame the "Thoughts" poems. The man, unlike the very young, unfallen child, can think, but his thoughts must be grounded in, circumscribed and contained by Love and Goodness, if he is to think rightly. Traherne is, as he called himself, "a Philosophical Poet," a divine philosopher as well as a poet, who puts great stock in right thinking, but above all in Love and its consequence, Goodness (see *CE,* pp. 84, 181). "Love" concerns the mutual love between God and man or, more precisely, between God and the "I" of the poem. In "Love" the right seer is singled out and raised up to "Drink the Cup." "Goodnesse" concerns man's love for his fellow man or, more specifically, Traherne's love for his fellow man. In "Goodnesse" Traherne, the poet-priest, implicitly offers the life-giving chalice to his fellow men, as indeed he does throughout (and by means of) the Dobell Folio; for, traditionally, after the soul tastes and is nourished by the joys of the contemplative life, it turns to the active life of working for the enlightenment and salvation of others, which work is itself joyful. The poems from "Love" to "Goodnesse" are Traherne's own distinctive microcosm of all that is embraced by the two great commandments of Christ: love thy God and love thy neighbor — total obedience to which leads directly and immediately to the joyful freedom of the Kingdom of Heaven here and now. These commandments express, in different terms, Traherne's central theme of becoming like unto a child — one who has "childlike" vision and love — for of such is the Kingdom of Heaven.

> What hinders then, but we in heav'n may be
> Even here on Earth did we but rightly see? (p. 180)

This couplet is from "Thoughts IV," a joyous hymn of praise, which follows "Desire" and makes one of many transitions in the Folio between "I" and "we." The second half of "Thoughts IV" contains all seven major classes of Traherne's pneuma-revealing symbols and, echoing I Corinthians 13:12, humbly concludes in Everyman's voice with a prayer for unitive vision. The "I" who has already attained to "The true Mysterious Depths of Blessedness" ("Love," p. 168) desires that "we" share his realized blessings:

> Fowls Fishes Beasts, Trees Herbs and precious flowers,
> Seeds Spices Gums and Aromatick Bowers,
> Wherwith we are enclos'd and servd, each day
> By his Appointment do their Tributes pay,
> And offer up themselvs as Gifts of Love,
> Bestowd on Saints, proceeding from above.
> Could we but justly, wisely, truly prize
> These Blessings, we should be above the Skies,
> And Praises sing with pleasant Heart and Voice,
> Adoring with the Angels should rejoyce.
> The fertile Clouds give Rain, the purer Air,
> Is Warm and Wholsom, Soft and Bright and fair.
> The Stars are Wonders which his Wisdom names,
> The Glorious Sun the Knowing Soul enflames.
> The very Heavens in their Sacred Worth,
> At once serv us, and set his Glory forth.
> Their Influences touch the Gratefull Sence,
> They pleas the Ey with their Magnificence.
> While in his Temple all his Saints do sing,
> And for his Bounty prais their Heavenly King.
> All these are in his Omnipresence still
> As Living Waters from his Throne they trill.

As Tokens of his Lov they all flow down,
Their Beauty Use and Worth the Soul do Crown.
Men are like Cherubims on either hand,
Whose flaming Love by his Divine Command,
Is made a Sacrifice to ours; which Streams
Throughout all Worlds, and fills them all with Beams.
We drink our fill, and take their Beauty in,
While Jesus Blood refines the Soul from Sin.
His Grievous Cross is a Supreme Delight,
And of all Heavenly ones the greatest Sight.
His Throne is neer, tis just before our face,
And all Eternitie his Dwelling place.
His Dwelling place is full of Joys and Pleasures,
His Throne a fountain of Eternal Treasures.
His Omnipresence is all Sight and Love,
Which whoso sees, he ever dwells above.
With soft Embraces it doth Clasp the Soul,
And Watchfully all Enemies controul.
It enters in, and doth a Temple find,
Or make a Living one within the Mind.
That while Gods Omnipresence in us lies,
His Treasures might be all before our Eys:
For Minds and Souls intent upon them here,
Do with the Seraphims abov appear:
And are like Spheres of Bliss, by Lov and Sight,
By Joy, Thanksgiving, Prais, made infinite.
O give me Grace to see thy face, and be
A constant Mirror of Eternitie.
Let my pure Soul, transformed to a Thought,
Attend upon thy Throne, and as it ought
Spend all its Time in feeding on thy Lov,
And never from thy Sacred presence mov.

> So shall my Conversation ever be
> In Heaven, and I O Lord my GOD with Thee! [21]

(pp. 181–182)

Images of nature's universal loving sacrifice for and service to man are followed by allusions to Christ's sacrificial-sacramental-redemptive life. Rightly apprehended, the entire perfect, natural world imitates Christ, the divine pattern and example, who is our food and drink. "We drink our fill." And dying to the life of ego and "feeding on thy Lov," man paradoxically best attends and serves God. Appropriately and inevitably, the next and last poem in the Dobell Folio also is a communion poem.[22]

For Traherne the Neoplatonist the form of the Good is the highest form, coinciding with the beautiful and the true and subsuming all other forms. Contemplation of it is the goal of the philosopher in *The Republic* and the lover in *The Symposium,* a goal attained, if attained at all, only after years of effort, intellectual training, and devotion. Plato regards the universe as an organic unity governed by a universal purpose, the form or ideal of the Good, the *logos*. But Traherne is first and foremost a Christian, which means that for him the active life aptly follows and crowns the contemplative life — "The Bliss of other Men is my Delight" — and especially that for him Christ is the primary and constant ideal, way, *Logos*. To manifest Goodness in love of other men is to manifest God, to become atoned, at one with Christ, for Christ is both Love and Goodness. Though one reads criticism to the contrary, Christ does pervade and inform the poems of the Dobell Folio, particularly if we see him as St. Paul did: the last Adam who is a quickening Spirit. Traherne refers to him sometimes overtly, most often subtly or indirectly, as in his major symbols. In "Desire" the reference to "his right

Hand" provides one of the links to "Thoughts IV," the epigraph of which is Psalm 16:11:

> In thy Presence there is fulness
> of Joy, and at thy right hand there
> are Pleasures for ever more.   (p. 179)

"When it is said that He sits on His Father's right hand," Julian of Norwich explains, "it means that He is in the highest nobility of His Father's joys"; to this English mystic "our good Lord showed His own Son and Adam to be but one man," and "by Adam I understand all men." [23] "Jesus Blood" most notably leads us to "Goodnesse," wherein the primary pneuma symbolism of "the Bleeding Vines" and "Wines" obtains. "I am the vine," Christ says, "ye are the branches: He that abideth in me, and I in him, the same bringeth forth much fruit: for without me ye can do nothing" (John 15:5).

The Soft and Swelling Grapes that on their Vines   2
  Receiv the Lively Warmth that Shines
    Upon them, ripen there for me:
      Or Drink they be
Or Meat. The Stars salute my pleased Sence
With a Derivd and borrowed Influence
    But better Vines do Grow
    Far Better Wines do flow
        Above, and while
        The Sun doth Smile
Upon the Lillies there, and all things warme
Their pleasant Odors do my Spirit charm.

> Their rich Affections do like precious Seas
>   Of Nectar and Ambrosia pleas.
> Their Eys are Stars, or more Divine:
>   And Brighter Shine
> Their Lips are soft and Swelling Grapes, their Tongues
> A Quire of Blessed and Harmonious Songs.
>   Their Bosoms fraught with Love
>   Are Heavens all Heavens above
> And being Images of GOD, they are
> The Highest Joys his Goodness did prepare.   (p. 184)

The attentive reader of Traherne's poems will readily recall many lines, literal catalogs, and appositions of symbolic images and phrases that reverberate with these last two stanzas of the Dobell Folio, such as "Those living Stars mine Eys," from "The Preparative." In "Goodnesse" (see also stanza 2), "Stars" is the traditional symbol for redeemed men, God's saints, as in Vaughan's poetry, too.[24] And from "The Person":

> My Tongue, my Eys,
> My cheeks, my Lips, my Ears, my Hands, my Feet,
>   Their Harmony is far more Sweet;
> Their Beauty true. And these in all my Ways
> Shall Themes becom, and Organs of thy Praise.   (p. 78)

In "Goodnesse," the individual Self has been expanded, has been joined by other Selves, to form a single choir or Communion of Saints united in praise of God, like Dante's hymn of all Paradise, to realize the Mystical Body of Christ, to become him (see *CE,* pp. 82–83 and I Cor. 12). Completed, successful spiritual journey always begins in a temple and ends in a Temple. The infant starts his life in "A House I knew not, newly clothd with Skin"

("The Preparative," p. 20); then, largely by means of "the Errors and the Wrongs That *Mortal Words* convey," his "foes puld down the Temple to the Ground" ("Dumnesse," pp. 40, 44); finally, the Living Temple is raised by the Silent Word into the Mystical Body of Christ ("Thoughts IV," ll. 75–94, and "Goodnesse"). The Dobell Folio sequence properly terminates in Agape, which, among other things, is a love feast, observed with scripture reading, prayers, and songs. "I speak as to wise men; judge ye what I say. The cup of blessing which we bless, is it not the communion of the blood of Christ? The bread which we break, is it not the communion of the body of Christ? For we being many are one bread, and one body: for we are all partakers of that one bread" (I Cor. 10:15–17; see also John 17:21–23). "And they, O my God, being, so delicious how can I chuse but love them as my self" ("Thanksgivings for God's Attributes," ll. 232–233 and see the following lines). "He thought that he was to treat evry man in the Person of Christ" (*C* IV 28). "Or Drink they be Or Meat." "Goodnesse" is an eating and drinking song and prayer, a communion hymn, a union poem. *Hoc est corpus meum. Tat tvam asi.*

The universal feasting portrayed in "The Circulation" and the universal serving and sacrificing shown in "Thoughts IV" may be seen through "Goodnesse" as a daily, constant eucharistic supper. With its eucharistic symbolism, "Goodnesse" reveals that the sacramental life is the everyday life; that the ordinary, apprehended with love, is extraordinary, joyous, miraculous, suffused with and illuminated by divinity. It is in redeemed "childhood" as it was in original innocent childhood:

> I felt a Vigour in my Sence
> That was all Spirit. I within did flow
> With Seas of Life, like Wine;

> I nothing in the World did know,
>   But 'twas Divine.   ("Wonder," p. 8)

Eckhart writes that "to know and to see how near God's Kingdom is, is to say with Jacob: 'God is in this place and I did not know it.' " [25] So Traherne says: "The World is a Mirror of infinit Beauty . . . It is the Paradice of God. It is more to Man since he is faln, then it was before. It is the Place of Angels, and the Gate of Heaven. When Jacob waked out of His Dream, he said, *God is here and I wist it not. How Dreadfull is this Place! This is none other, then the Hous of God, and the Gate of Heaven*" (*C* I 31). In the *Thanksgivings,* Traherne prays "to know the Love of Christ which passeth Knowledge; that we may be filled with all the fulness of God"; for love is His blessed laws and the key to the gate of Heaven (II, 270f). "When you lov men, the World Quickly becometh yours . . . certainly He that Delights not in Lov makes vain the Univers" (*C* II 64, 65). "The best Principle whereby a man can stear his course in this World . . . is to love every man in the whole World, as GOD doth. For this will make a man the Image of GOD, and fill him with the mind and spirit of Christ" (*CE*, p. 253).[26] Traherne's love for his fellow men, everywhere apparent and in "Goodnesse" so very obvious, is the fruit of his clear vision of them as vines or as branches of the true Vine, whose commandment is "that ye love one another, as I have loved you" (John 15:12). On another occasion, Jacob struggled all night and when the light came he was blessed, he became Israel, and he "called the name of the place Peniel: for I have seen God face to face, and my life is preserved" (Gen. 32:30). "O give me Grace to see thy face, and be A Constant Mirror of Eternitie" (p. 182), Traherne's assumed voice in "Thoughts IV" humbly implores God, Whose "Throne is near, tis just before our face" (p. 181); and through his achieved vision he continues in "Goodnesse," "The Face of God is Goodness unto all" (p. 182). Thus, looking full into the eyes of men and seeing then face to face, Traherne perceived

> The Light which on ten thousand faces Shines
> The Beams which crown ten thousand Vines
> With Glory and Delight,   (p. 183)

and, silently contemplating the Eternal Spring of the very good creation, he found in these "Images of God," for whom he wrote, labored, lived, and whom he loved, "The Highest Joys his Goodness did prepare.

Appendix A. Traherne and Renaissance Poetic Theory and Practice

APART FROM NOTING HIS AFFINITIES to certain Romantic poets, standard critical practice begins and ends by placing Traherne among the English metaphysical poets of the seventeenth century without specifying in what sense he is "metaphysical." As a beginning, this practice may be helpful and valid because Traherne's poetry does share certain characteristics in common with poets like Herbert and Vaughan and because Traherne's poetic practice may be accurately described by and included under one or another theory of metaphysical poetry — to say nothing of the fact that Traherne's poetry is more metaphysical, in the ordinary meaning of the word, than Donne's. Among the various theories of metaphysical poetry and metaphysical wit, perhaps the most useful insights into Traherne's poetry and poetic practice are to be found in the speculations of certain Renaissance theorists, such as Giordano Bruno, Baltasar Gracian, and Emmanuele Tesauro. The questions whether and to what extent Traherne knew such theorists cannot be answered with certainty. A full discussion of their views would require lengthy development and numerous qualifying exceptions; all we need to do here, however, is to suggest the relevance of a few of their central ideas to Traherne.[1]

God, according to these theorists, is the divine wit, creator of a unified, well-ordered universe. The poetic faculty in man, identified with "wit" (synonymous with the French *génie* and *esprit*), is a vestige of God in the human being: "whatever the world has of wit either is God or is from God."[2] By means of this gift of wit, this light derived from Heaven, which was dissociated from the discursive and logical faculties, the poet discovers and creates universal correspondences, expresses the underlying unity of all things. He is a human wit whose poetic act is imitative of the divine creative act and whose purpose is to reveal the unity and order, and thus the beauty, of all God's creation. This is to say that the final answer to the question "what truth does the metaphysical or witty poem reveal?" is that "the poem instructs and delights with the presentation of an exquisitely ordered universe." [3]

How might this purpose be better accomplished than by writing a unified sequence of poems? Context is exceptionally significant in Traherne because of his conceptions of beauty ("Order the Beauty even of Beauty is" — "The Vision," p. 26) and of the essential self, the isolated ego being a fiction, an illusion, a lesser reality — the glitter of the sun, D. H. Lawrence has said, on the surface of the waters. "The Preparative," "My Spirit," and other poems show that it is the act, the "connection" between subject and object, which is ultimately real; the individual man is real not in isolation from but in relation to the rest of the world and God, dependent upon that relationship for his full meaning, value, being. So it is with the individual line and poem in respect to other lines and poems in the sequence. Traherne has an extraordinarily profound sense of order and wholeness about his poetry and about the self and the world. In a fundamental and pervasive way, there is, again, a vital connection between, an organic oneness of, form and content.

As for metaphor itself, "the true metaphor was brief, intense, and established a remarkable identity." [4] Although Traherne's poetry is not conceited or metaphorical in a typically metaphysical or Donnean sense, Traherne seems to have applied this idea in an unusually thoroughgoing way, making his metaphors even briefer by concentrating them into symbols, then using these symbols in intense appositions, and, finally, establishing largely by means of these symbols the remarkable "identity" of the finite and the infinite. Moreover, the nonlogical character of wit or imagination (according to Tesauro, wit is always logically fallacious) may help to account for Traherne's characteristic paradoxical mode. And Traherne's exuberant, appositive style, often snatching graces beyond the reach of art, blossoming from his own joy of living, and being exactly correlative with his content of Felicity, corresponds to or develops out of the "furor poeticus," which the theorists introduced to support the view that poetry is the result of a special state of the human spirit.

The principle of universal analogy as a poetic, or the poetic of correspondences, accords with the Renaissance world picture and its familiar correspondences. More particularly, even though that world picture was changing radically in Traherne's day, such a poetic is suitable for Traherne because, however much he may have consciously used or modified it in his poetic practice, it harmonizes with certain of his theological and cosmological views: everything is of or from God, who is the fountain, means, end; there is a divine element in man; God's universe is, as the doctrine of the Golden Mean promulgates, a well-ordered, wholly interrelated and beautiful unity, and to see this is essential to attaining Felicity; and, according to Traherne's epistemology, right apprehension or perception is an imaginative, creative act, and a gift of grace.

A critic may rightly and profitably begin, then, by regarding Traherne's poetry as metaphysical in the sense just outlined above as well as in the sense that Traherne is most near akin to the "metaphysical" Herbert and Vaughan. But he must not end there. In addition to biblical and contemplative influences, previously discussed, a fuller appreciation of Traherne's poetry might also take into account the analogies to, even possible influences of, the "native vein" of writers apparently alluded to in "The Author to the Critical Peruser":

> An easy Stile drawn from a native vein,
> A clearer Stream than that which Poets feign,
> Whose bottom may, how deep so'ere, be seen,
> Is that which I think fit to win Esteem.   (p. 2)

Besides being consistent with Traherne's eschewing "curling Metaphors" and possibly echoing the pre-Augustan Denham, might these lines (assuming that Traherne means some or many, rather than all, "Poets") point if not to Chaucer's couplet form and the medieval religious, didactic lyric, then to such Renaissance poets as Wyatt, Sidney, Spenser, and Jonson, and perhaps even to Milton, who published his early poems in 1645 and the first edition of *Paradise Lost* in 1667? The first thirty lines of Milton's "At a Vacation Exercise" (published a year before Traherne's death), in which Milton resolves to express his "naked thoughts" in his "native Language," especially bear close comparison to Traherne with respect to diction and rhyme as well as theme. Are the feigning, unclear poets the metaphysicals in the profane line of Donne or those influenced by continental models? Would Traherne have closely associated Herbert and Vaughan with Donne or, rather, is not the notion of their deep indebtedness to Donne a much later one, and one that recent studies have begun to question?

As one critic has argued, Wyatt's poetic style is related to and grows out of the medieval, plain, "contemplative," lyric tradition, a "native vein" Traherne would naturally be responsive to; and, as another critic writes, Wyatt's psalms touch "at times the mystical vision which to Blake was the only domain of poetry and the only reality of life," a vision akin to Traherne's.[5] Furthermore, a list of Jonsonian poetic qualities reads like a description of some features of Traherne's poetry: sincerity, plainness, lucidity, precision, directness of language, economy of utterance, sense of structure and underlying symmetry, and naked dignity of style. Jonson's authoritative couplets helped to establish the couplet in form and purpose as it was to continue through the seventeenth century. Traherne, we should note, makes considerable use of the couplet form. Five of the Dobell Folio poems are written in heroic couplets, and couplets of varying lengths contribute to the shape of the stanzaic pattern in many other D and F poems. Although no critic would regard Traherne as a Spenserian in the manner of Giles and Phineas Fletcher, George Wither, or William Browne, and although Jonson charged Spenser with having "writ no language" and Traherne conceivably might have included him among the feigning poets, some Spenserian qualities nevertheless do seem evident in Traherne's poetry, and the earlier Christian Neoplatonist would have had special appeal for the later one. Finally, if we cannot with certainty say that Traherne directly learned metrical ingenuity and a certain kind of "pure simplicity," plainness and directness, as well as cataloging and apposition, from, among others, such an influential "native" Elizabethan poet and translator of the Psalms as Sir Philip Sidney, he would have been aware of these qualities and devices, probably derivative partly from Sidney, in Herbert's poetry.[6]

Much of this discussion of a "native vein" remains conjectural, none of it is intended to imply that Traherne is more Spenserian or Miltonic than metaphysical, and many important differences do of course exist between Traherne's "Stile" and the poetry of Wyatt, Sidney, Spenser, Jonson, and Milton. Although the myth of the Fall is also central in Spenser and Milton, Traherne is, let me emphasize, rather more metaphysical than Spenserian or Miltonic and closest, stylistically as well as thematically, to Herbert and Vaughan. But a thoughtful evaluation of Traherne must not merely label him as belonging to this or that school nor merely impute him a lesser member of the school. By pointing to the value and necessity of considering various poets and poetic traditions, this brief discussion may help to underscore the uniqueness and distinctiveness of Traherne, a poet who is no simple imitator but who, just as he read widely in philosophy and theology, may well have drawn widely on much previous poetry from the Bible to his own contemporaries and who yet attains his own remarkable voice and style.

Appendix B. Traherne and the Perennial Philosophy

In his study of *Mysticism,* F. C. Happold observes that "not only have mystics been found in all ages, in all parts of the world and in all religious systems, but also mysticism has manifested itself in similar or identical forms wherever the mystical consciousness has been present. Because of this it has sometimes been called the Perennial Philosophy." [1] After Traherne has been fully and properly understood within the context and through the perspective of his own Christian mystical tradition it would then be appropriate and most interesting and fruitful, I believe, either to discuss the "similar or identical forms" to be found in his work, to see him, that is, in the context of worldwide mysticism, or, shifting the focus to a different kind of study, to determine precisely what contributions his work makes to the subject of the Perennial Philosophy. These difficult, challenging studies would be greatly facilitated by the many excellent recent works on comparative mysticism and on the Perennial Philosophy by distinguished authors such as Ananda Coomaraswamy, Mircea Eliade, Aldous Huxley, Thomas Merton, Sidney Spencer, W. T. Stace, D. T. Suzuki, and Alan Watts, to name a few. That Traherne particularly would lend himself to such studies and that he is frequently cited by writers on the subjects of worldwide and comparative mysticism I take as signs and consequences of his outstanding mystical genius and of his considerable stature as a Perennial Philosopher. Although, for example, Traherne appears to have had no direct substantial knowledge of Buddhism whatsover, the parallels of paradoxicality, spontaneity, and joyful zest and humor, among others, to be observed in his writings and in the literature of Zen are indeed remarkable, whatever the final explanation may be. As notes toward the kinds of studies just mentioned and as a way of further suggesting the dignity and universality of Traherne's theme of childhood or his tradition's story of the Fall, I should like briefly to bring to bear several points of view — the mythic, metaphysical, historical-scientific, and psychoanalytical. Doing so should also broaden, deepen, and sharpen our understanding of that theme and story. Again, "Our Saviors Meaning, when He said, He must be Born again and becom a little Child that will enter into the Kingdom of Heaven: is Deeper far then is generaly believed" (*Centuries* III 5).

In the widest sense, the Dobell Folio poems may be understood in terms of the "monomyth" of the hero's journey. Joseph Campbell points out that, characteristically, the journey is divided into three stages: departure, initiation, and return. The hero goes forth into an extraordinary world; there he encounters fabulous forces and wins a decisive victory; he returns from his adventures with a boon for mankind. Such is the spiritual progress of the archetypal hero from Apollo to Jesus to Wotan. He is the one who can overcome personal and social limitations, come in contact or communion with the source of life, from which his vision springs; transformed, reborn, he then teaches his fellow men the lesson he has learned of life renewed. The journey is a symbolic one, for the godly powers sought and won are not discovered or attained ones but "lost" or "forgotten" ones which are rediscovered, reattained, and "within the heart of the hero all the time. He is . . . 'God's son,' who has learned to know how much that title means. From this point of view the hero is symbolical of that divine creative and redemptive image which is hidden within us all, only waiting to be known and rendered into life." [2]

"The story of 'lost and found,' of death and resurrection, of self-forgetting and self-discovery, is perhaps the most common theme of mythological and religious symbolism."[3] In the Christian religion, this story is of course the central one of the Creation, Fall, and Redemption, which, symbolically understood, is, as we have seen, the theme of childhood in the Dobell poems. From a religious, metaphysical point of view, Alan Watts shows that this theme may be regarded as a threefold progress from unconsciousness through ego-consciousness to Self-consciousness. The first stage is one of unconscious union of the finite with the infinite. For the union to become conscious, the third stage, there must be a period of conscious division, the second stage. "To learn to appreciate his home, the Prodigal Son had to be separated from it, to travel into the loneliness and dereliction of a far country. Similarly, the Self emerges into consciousness as the separate and lonely ego, for by this means it 'comes to itself' like the Son in the parable, and begins the journey back to conscious union with the Father."[4] Odysseus finally arrives home in Ithaca not in spite of but *because of* his wanderings. And as a modern Ulysses learned, the longest way round is the shortest way home. Or, one learns that in the ultimate sense he has never left and can never leave Home, that he can never escape his Father's love. In short, the Fall is fortunate. There must be a Fall so that one can rediscover, consciously learn and thoroughly value, his being God's son, to which fact the Incarnation myth is the greatest Christian testimony.

From a historical-scientific point of view, the pioneer psychologist R. M. Bucke similarly regards the progress of both racial and individual human life as a movement from Simple Consciousness through Self-Consciousness to Cosmic Consciousness. (Though their terminology differs Bucke and Watts mean essentially the same thing.) According to Bucke, children under, say, three years old and animals have Simple Consciousness; they are conscious of perceived objects without knowing they are conscious of them, and they have no consciousness of themselves as distinct entities. Bucke's Self-consciousness is consciousness of oneself as a distinct entity apart from the rest of the universe, and the knowledge that one is conscious of an object. Such consciousness is acquired and characterized by conceptual thinking and the use of language; in fact, Bucke refers to language as the "other self" of Self-consciousness. The meaning of Cosmic Consciousness constitutes the burden of Bucke's entire volume. But, briefly, Cosmic Consciousness is the "highest happiness"; it "shows the cosmos to consist not of dead matter governed by unconscious, rigid, and unintending law; it shows it on the contrary as entirely immaterial, entirely spiritual and entirely alive; it shows that death is an absurdity, that every one and everything has eternal life; it shows that the universe is God and that God is the universe, and that no evil ever did or ever will enter into it; a great deal of this is, of course, from the point of self-consciousness, absurd — it is nevertheless undoubtedly true." [5] Indeed, these ideas, some of which Traherne shares, need many qualifications and explanations, which Bucke proceeds to present, if they are to appear other than merely hyperbolic.

Finally, what we have just been saying in mythic, metaphysical, and historical-scientific terms receives treatment from a psychoanalytical point of view in Norman O. Brown's reinterpretation and extension of Freud, *Life Against Death*. The whole of Brown's study repeatedly reveals that psychoanalysis confirms age-old religious experience and is in fact the heir to a mystical tradition which it must affirm. Essentially, Brown contends that repression, which Freud regarded as the basis of civilization, results in both individual and social neurosis, in "the disease called man" (one is reminded of Traherne's poem from *Christian*

Ethicks, "Mankind is sick" and of his premise in *Centuries* IV 20, that to think the world a Bedlam and one self a physician is a necessary step on the way to Happiness). The remedy, the abolition of repression, is variously referred to as Dionysian mysticism, the recovery of childhood, or, in traditional Christian terms, "The Resurrection of the Body," the title of Brown's last chapter. Brown's categories marking the individual and historical progress of man (primal unity, differentiation through antagonism, final harmony) are analogous to — it is not inaccurate to say fundamentally identical with — the threefold stages of Watts and Bucke: "the history of mankind consists in a departure from a condition of undifferentiated primal unity with himself and with nature, an intermediate period in which man's powers are developed through differentiation and antagonism (alienation) with himself and with nature, and a final return to a unity on a higher level or harmony." The pertinence of all of this to Traherne is sufficiently suggested in Brown's central contention that "the only grounds for hope for humanity are in the facts of human childhood; and psychoanalysis is nothing without the doctrine that mankind is that species of animal which has the immortal project of recovering its own childhood." [6]

Notes
Index

Abbreviations Used in Citations

ELH	Journal of English Literary History
JHI	Journal of the History of Ideas
MLN	Modern Language Notes
MLQ	Modern Language Quarterly
MLR	Modern Language Review
N&Q	Notes and Queries
SP	Studies in Philology

Notes

Introduction

1. *Thomas Traherne: Centuries, Poems, and Thanksgivings* (Oxford, 1958), I, xv.

2. *The Poetical Works of Thomas Traherne, B.D.* (London, 1903). Philip Traherne had also made some changes in the Dobell Folio itself. Dobell unavoidably printed some of these. Though significant, they are, fortunately, far fewer and generally less destructive than the changes which Philip had perpetrated in the British Museum MS. Burney 392. In his edition, Margoliouth restored to the Dobell Folio, whenever possible, Thomas' own text. In referring to the "Dobell Folio," I mean only the poems contained in the first part of that MS (2r, 3v–16r) and not the larger second part, the "Commonplace Book" (16v–96r). See Margoliouth, I, xii–xiv, and Carol L. Marks, "Thomas Traherne's Commonplace Book," *The Papers of the Bibliographical Society of America,* 58 (1964): 458–465.

3. Oxford, 1910, pp. xxviii–xxvix.

4. My photostatic copy of Burney MS. 392 shows extensive crossing out and rewriting in "Churches II" as compared to most of the other poems. Philip apparently made most of his revisions before (or while) copying the poems onto this MS.

5. Some examples of the kind of criticism just discussed are the following: Louise Willcox, "A Joyous Mystic," *The North American Review,* 191 (1911): p. 900; J. W. Proud, "Thomas Traherne: A Divine Philosopher," *Friends' Quarterly Examiner,* 51 (January 1917): 71; Arthur Quiller-Couch, *Studies in Literature,* First Series (Cambridge, 1918), p. 153, and *Felicities of Thomas Traherne* (London, 1934), pp. xiii–xix; S. T. H. Parker, "The Riches of Thomas Traherne," *The Living Age,* 314 (July 22, 1922): 225; Ernst Christ, *Studien zu Thomas Traherne* (Tübingen, 1932), pp. 47–60, esp. pp. 56–58; Q. Iredale, *Thomas Traherne* (Oxford, 1935), pp. 61–62; Norman Ault, *Seventeenth Century Lyrics from the Original Texts* (New York, 1928,

1950), p. 513; Douglas Bush, *English Literature in the Earlier Seventeenth Cenutry, 1600–1660* (Oxford, 1945), p. 148; Margaret Willy, *Life Was Their Cry* (London, 1950), p. 83. The most complete bibliography of Traherne criticism is my "Thomas Traherne: A Chronological Bibliography," *The Library Chronicle*, forthcoming.

6. "The Manuscripts of the Poems of Thomas Traherne," *MLR*, 26 (1931): 407. And see *The Poetical Works of Thomas Traherne* (London, 1932), pp. x–xii, 249.

7. *Thomas Traherne: A Critical Biography* (Princeton and Oxford, 1944), pp. 194, 196. A most recent version of this same form-content criticism is to be found in K. W. Salter, *Thomas Traherne: Mystic and Poet* (London, 1964), p. 119.

8. *The Poetical Works*, p. lxx.

9. Denonain, *Thèmes et Formes de la Poésie "Metaphysique"* (Paris, 1956), pp. 254f; Wallace, "Thomas Traherne and the Structure of Meditation," *ELH*, 25 (June 1958): 80, 81.

10. New Haven, 1964, pp. 35–102. See esp. pp. 22–23 for a description of the basic difference between Augustinian and Ignatian meditation.

11. See Helen Gardner's review of *The Poetry of Meditation* in *Review of English Studies*, 8 (1957): 194–200, and Stanley Archer, "Meditation and the Structure of Donne's 'Holy Sonnets,'" *ELH*, 28 (1961): 137–147.

12. Wallace, "Structure of Meditation," pp. 81, 88.

13. General studies of mysticism which include Traherne are the following: W. K. Fleming, *Mysticism in Christianity* (London, 1913), pp. 190–193; Caroline F. E. Spurgeon, *Mysticism in English Literature* (Cambridge, England, 1913), pp. 76–80; E. Herman, *The Meaning and Value of Mysticism*, 3rd ed. (New York, 1925), pp. 207–213, 219–220; Geraldine E. Hodgson, *English Mystics* (London, 1922), pp. 246–259, 294–301; Rufus M. Jones, *Spiritual Reformers in the 16th and 17th Centuries* (London, 1914), pp. 323–335; Evelyn Underhill, *The Mystics of the Church* (London, 1925), pp. 221–222; Percy H. Osmond, *The Mystical Poets of the English Church* (New York, 1919), pp. 234–249; Gerald Bullet, *The English Mystics* (London, 1950), pp. 110–112; F. C. Happold, *Mysticism* (Baltimore, 1963), pp. 93, 126, 128, 336–344; Sidney Spencer, *Mysticism in World Religion* (Baltimore, 1963), pp.

290–291, 295; Thomas Merton, *Mystics and Zen Masters* (New York, 1967), pp. 129, 132–134. The many "appreciations" of or introductions to Traherne need not be listed here.

14. Leishman, *The Metaphysical Poets* (Oxford, 1934), p. 192; Gilbert, "Thomas Traherne as Artist," *MLQ*, 8 (1947): 436–442, a section entitled "The Metaphor of Childhood."

15. On the matter of his supposed subjectivism and egocentrism, see, for example, the several longer studies of Traherne's mystical philosophy: Elbert Thompson, "The Philosophy of Thomas Traherne," *Philological Quarterly*, 8 (1929): 100, 101, 106, 109, and "Mysticism in 17th-Century English Literature," *SP*, 18 (1921): 189, 208, 209; Itrat Husain, *The Mystical Element in the Metaphysical Poets of the Seventeenth Century* (London, 1948), pp. 283–284; Robert Ellrodt, *L'Inspiration personnelle et l'esprit du temps chez les poètes métaphysiques anglais*, pt. I, vol. II (Paris, 1960), pp. 282–286, 310, 342, 348. But cf. Martz's just conclusion on the *Centuries* and Augustine's *Confessions*: "Both works are ultimately theocentric, not egocentric." *The Paradise Within*, p. 41.

16. "Select Meditations": The Fourth Century, 66; several prose passages and two poems on humility follow a longer section on the cardinal and theological virtues and conclude the MS. For the suggestion that the "Select Meditations" is an early work of Traherne's, written perhaps between 1660 and 1665, see James Osborn's article announcing the discovery, "A New Traherne Manuscript," *TLS*, October 8, 1964, p. 928.

17. For example, Husain, *The Mystical Element*, pp. 274, 297–299; Ellrodt, *Poètes Métaphysiques*, pp. 333–334, 339, 363, 371, 375; and Wallace, *MLN*, 74 (1959), 748. (Cf. Husain, p. 266, with Wade's *Thomas Traherne*, pp. 216, 220, 221.)

18. K. W. Salter, *Thomas Traherne: Mystic and Poet* (London, 1964), pp. 92–100; quotations from 92, 93, 46. Cf. Joan Webber: "Communicating through the psalms, David reaches communion and union with God just as Traherne does in his *Centuries*." "'I and Thou' in the Prose of Thomas Traherne," *Papers on English Language and Literature*, 2 (1966): 260.

19. Salter, *Thomas Traherne*, pp. 111–121; quotations from p. 119. Since many of the other serious defects and weaknesses of Salter's

book have been pointed out in reviews, they need not be repeated here: see, for example, Carol L. Marks, *Renaissance News,* 19 (1966): 60–62, and R. L. Colie, *English Language Notes,* 3 (1965): 70–71.

Chapter One

1. For a supplementary discussion of "Traherne and the Perennial Philosophy" see Appendix B.

2. See, for example, Evelyn Underhill, *Mysticism* (New York, 1955); William Ralph Inge, *Christian Mysticism,* 3rd ed. (London, 1913); Rufus M. Jones, *Studies in Mystical Religion* (London, 1936); Ray C. Petry, ed., *Late Medieval Mysticism* (Philadelphia, 1957); Charles B. Schmitt, "Perennial Philosophy: From Agostino Steuco to Leibniz," *JHI,* 27 (1966): 505–532; and some of the general studies of mysticism referred to in the Introduction, n. 13. Since our primary object is to examine Traherne's thought and art and not to present a history of mysticism, the differences among the contemplatives of his tradition need not be of direct concern to us.

Most recently, Malcolm M. Day, by adopting essentially this same approach to Traherne that I first proposed in a previous article, as he notes, has successfully resolved the critically vexed issue of Traherne's view of pre-existence. See his "Traherne and the Doctrine of Pre-existence," *SP,* 65 (January 1968): 81–97.

3. *Centuries* III 2, for example, in Margoliouth, I, 110. Hereafter *Centuries* is abbreviated as *C.*

4. See, for example, *C* III 27f, esp. 66: "but as I read the Bible I was here and there Surprized with such Thoughts and found by degrees that these things had been written of before, not only in the Scriptures but in many of the fathers and that this was the Way of Communion with God."

By a further refinement, such as dividing the third stage into two "redeemed" states (in this life and in the afterlife, generally speaking) or adding between the second and third stages one other stage (which in general shares characteristics of both the second and third stages), many writers distinguish a fourfold pattern intead of or in addition to the more traditional threfold pattern. In several of his works, Traherne himself also refers to the "fourfold Estate of Innocency, Misery,

Grace, and Glory" (*C* III 43). For a list of such references in Traherne, see *Christian Ethicks,* ed. Carol Marks and George Guffey (Ithaca, 1968), p. 307, hereafter referred to as *CE*. This scholarly edition appeared just in time for me to adopt its text and change page references accordingly.

5. Underhill, *Mysticism,* p. 122.

6. "The state of progressive unification, in which we receive 'grace upon grace,' as we learn more and more of the 'fulness' of Christ, is called by the evangelist, in the verse just quoted and elsewhere, eternal life. This life is generally spoken of as a present possession rather than a future hope. 'He that believeth on the Son *hath* everlasting life'; 'he *is passed* from death unto life'; 'we *are* in Him that is true, even Jesus Christ. This *is* the true God, and eternal life.' " Inge, *Christian Mysticism,* p. 52. (Eternity is not more and more time but a present timelessness. "Eternity is a Mysterious Absence of Times and Ages"; *C* V 7.) See also Matt. 19:14 and John 3:3–5.

7. Luke 9: 24–25 in the translation of the recent *New English Bible* reads: "Whoever cares for his own safety is lost; but if a man will let himself be lost for my sake that man is safe. What will a man gain by winning the whole world, at the cost of his true self?" Several other New Testament passages in the Authorized Version of 1611, available of course to Traherne, make the distinction between soul and spirit quite plainly: for example, Heb. 4:12 and I Cor. 15:45. The Old Testament also provides important scriptural authority in, for example, Gen. 1:27 and Eccl. 12:7. Rom. 7:22, 2 Cor. 4:16, and Eph. 3:16 refer to the outward and inward or inner man; Col. 3:9, 10 to the old and new man.

There are several meanings of the complex terms *psyche, pneuma, nefesh,* and *ruach* which are not strictly germane to our discussion. For a convenient compilation of the many biblical meanings of these terms, see John L. McKenzie, S.J., *Dictionary of the Bible* (Milwaukee, 1965), s.v. soul and spirit, pp. 836–839 and 840–845. Unlike their rough English equivalents, soul and spirit, the terms *psyche* and *pneuma,* after they are defined in this chapter, will not carry ambiguous, irrelevant, and distracting meanings for the modern reader of English. Along with *soma* (body), these terms indicate St. Paul's trichotomous conception of man's nature, a conception which Traherne shares (see esp. *C* I 93–94).

8. Inge, *Christian Mysticism*, p. 6.

9. *De incarn. verbi*, 54, iii, cited in Alan W. Watts, *Behold the Spirit* (New York, 1947), p. 134; and see Augustine, *Confessions*, VII, x. On the region of unlikeness, see also *Meister Eckhart: Selected Treatises and Sermons*, ed. James M. Clark and John V. Skinner (London, 1958), p. 254.

10. *CE*, pp. 285–286. Traherne's distinction (pp. 231–232) between Soul and Mind parallels the distinction between pneuma and psyche or inward and outward man. Traherne frequently uses *Soul* (where we would use *Spirit*) to mean pneuma. He also uses *Soul* in a sense comparable to the Plotinian Soul, the third hypostasis.

11. Henri Bremond, *Prayer and Poetry*, tr. Algar Thorold (London, 1927), pp. 108–109; St. Catherine of Genoa is cited in Aldous Huxley, *The Perennial Philosophy* (London, 1946), p. 18; *Meister Eckhart: A Modern Translation*, tr. Raymond Bernard Blakney (New York, 1957), p. 180; Eckhart variously refers to pneuma as "the little castle," "the tabernacle of the Spirit," "the Light of the Spirit," "a spark" (*fünkelein*); Jan van Ruysbroeck, *The Spiritual Espousals*, tr. Eric Colledge (London, 1952), pp. 187–188. For additional examples, see Inge, *Christian Mysticism*, Appendix C, "The Doctrine of Deification"; R. A. Durr's discussion of "The Idea of the Divine Spark, or Seed" in *On the Mystical Poetry of Henry Vaughan* (Cambridge, Mass., 1962), Appendix A; and Eckhart's "The Nobleman" in Clark, *Meister Eckhart*, pp. 149–159.

12. Margoliouth, II, 54. Unless otherwise noted, all quotations of Traherne's poetry are from vol. II of the Margoliouth edition.

13. Compare, for example, Eckhart, in Blakney, *Meister Eckhart*, p. 303: "A holy soul is one with God, according to John 17:21, *That they all may be one in us, even as we are one.* Still, the creature is not the creator, nor is the just man God." Needless to say, I do not claim that Traherne was familiar with the Chhandogya Upanishad, in which the expression "tat tvam asi" appears. I use the expression merely as a convenient short-hand for a fundamental mystical idea found in Plato, Plotinus, Augustine, Eckhart, and many other writers whom Traherne may have known.

14. It is interesting to note that Eckhart derives *homo* from *humus* and *humilitas;* see, for example, Clark, *Meister Eckhart*, pp. 155, 200.

15. Blakney, *Meister Eckhart,* p. 129. See also p. 205: "As I have often said, there is something in the soul so closely akin to God that it is already one with him and need never be united to him."

16. *The Confessions* of Saint Augustine, tr. Edward B. Pusey (New York, 1949), p. 44. And see *The Life of St. Teresa:* "He seemed to be so near"; and the seventeenth-century *Light on the Candlestick:* "God is nearer unto every man than himself, because He penetrates the most inward and intimate parts of man, and is the Life of the inmost spirit." Both quoted in Sidney Spencer, *Mysticism in World Religion* (Baltimore, 1963), pp. 243, 279. See also "Thanksgiving for God's Attributes," ll. 242–244.

17. Aquinas, *Summa Theologica,* II–II, 122, 2, 1, and cf. his *De Veritate* (2, 1, 9) and *Contra Gentiles* (bk. 1, ch. 5); *Franz Pfeiffer's Meister Eckhart,* tr. C. de. B. Evans (London, 1924), pp. 247, 64, and see also pp. 59–64; Ruysbroeck, *The Adornment of the Spiritual Marriage,* tr. C. A. Wynschenck (London, 1916), pp. 177–178; Jacob Boehme, *Six Theosophic Points and Other Writings,* tr. J. R. Earle (Ann Arbor, 1958), p. xxii; Henry Suso, *Little Book of Truth,* tr. James M. Clark (New York, n.d.), pp. 178, 191–192.

18. Against the contention of critics like Itrat Husain and Robert Ellrodt that negative theology is absent from Traherne, cf. Rosalie Colie's recent *Paradoxia Epidemica* (Princeton, 1966), pp. 145–168, which devotes a convincing chapter, "Affirmations in the Negative Theology: The Infinite," to Traherne as one "of the many Renaissance poets who . . . turned to poetic account the traditions of the negative theology."

19. For example, Paul Tillich, "The Religious Symbol," in *Symbolism in Religion and Literature,* ed. Rollo May (New York, 1960), p. 91; Underhill, *Mysticism,* ch. VI, "Mysticism and Symbolism," esp. p. 126; and W. T. Stace, *Time and Eternity* (Princeton, 1952), chs. 4 and 6.

20. This quotation expresses a Christian-Aristotelian rather than Platonic view insofar as we understand Plato as asserting the separation of Forms and matter and Aristotle as insisting upon the fusion of the universal form with the particular material thing into the complete unity of the individual. In *C* III 20, Traherne goes on to refer explicitly to "Golden Mean," and it is for this reason also that I designate the position here under discussion as the doctrine of the Golden Mean.

To judge from *C* III 20–21, a "Real Infinity" is not that which is "infinit in Bulk" but that which is infinite in "Profit Splendor . . . Delight."

21. R. B. Blakney in his *Meister Eckhart* translates Eckhart's "Nu" as "Now-moment" and suggests some of its meaning and tradition when he explains (p. xi) that it is "the point of division between the past and future — without duration — and yet the locus of eternity . . . See also Psalm 90:4; Augustine, *Confessions* XI, 16 and 20; Plato, *Timaeus* 37b." Also *C* V 7 and *CE*, pp. 67–69.

22. Esp. *C* I 7f, II 7–24, 93–100, III 18–21; *CE*, ch. 23 and pp. 53–54, 82–83; and "Thanksgivings for the Body" and "Thanksgivings for the Glory of God's Works." *Meditations on the Six Days of the Creation,* based on Genesis 1, has for its central theme the "Excellency of the Creation" and thus it is all quite relevant; particularly interesting and pertinent passages occur on pp. 13, 23, 32–33, 45, 57, 68, 70, and 84 of *A Collection of Meditations and Devotions in Three Parts* (London, 1717), of which *Meditations on the Six Days of the Creation* is Part I. The most recent and convincing study of the authorship of Parts I and II — Part III is a collection of devotional writings from various authors — is Catherine Owen's "The Authorship of the 'Meditations on the Six Days of Creation' and the 'Meditations and Devotions on the Life of Christ,' " *MLR*, 56 (January 1961): 1–12. In my study, I have drawn only on *Meditations on the Six Days of the Creation,* for I agree with Miss Owen's conclusion that only this work may be ascribed to Traherne with confidence.

In 1966, the Augustan Reprint Society reprinted *Meditations on the Six Days of the Creation,* with an Introduction by George Robert Guffey, so that this fine work is now easily and inexpensively available. Guffey's Introduction gives additional arguments for Traherne's authorship.

Chapter Two

1. Whatever else they have said, most critics have remarked about and responded to, in one way or another, this joy in Traherne's poetry. In effect, they have perhaps unknowingly implied Traherne to be a more successful poet than they have consciously realized or overtly indicated.

2. See esp. "Jordan II" ("Curling with metaphors a plain intention") and "Dulnesse" ("And with quaint metaphors her curled hair/Curl o're again"). The view that Traherne read and knew *The Temple* is supported by verbal echoes of Herbert throughout Traherne's poetry as well as Traherne's copy of Herbert's "To All Angels and Saints," entitled "A Hymne to all Saints out of Herbert" in the Church's Year-Book (Bodleian MS. Eng. th. e. 51). The comparison I have made between "A Hymne to all Saints out of Herbert" in my photostatic copy of the Church's Year-Book, f. 112v, and "To All Angels and Saints" in *The Works of George Herbert* (Oxford, 1959), pp. 77–78, shows that the differences between the two are very few and minor, such as Traherne may have made in a hasty copying or as may have appeared in the edition he used, though it is notable that Traherne, as is his practice, capitalizes more frequently. At least nine editions of *The Temple* were printed by 1667 and a tenth in 1674.

For the fullest account of the Church's Year-Book see Carol L. Marks, "Traherne's Church's Year-Book," *The Papers of the Bibliographical Society of America,* 60 (1966): 31–72.

3. In its context, "concealed" does not seem to make complete good sense. Was this word Philip's substitute for Thomas' "revealed"? My photostatic copy of British Museum Ms. Burney 392 shows only the faintest hint of an erasure. But Philip may have made a revision before copying it onto F.

4. D. T. Suzuki, *Mysticism: Christian and Buddhist* (New York, 1962), p. 81.

5. Cited in Alan W. Watts, *The Spirit of Zen* (New York, 1958), p. 78. Cf. Whitman in "Starting from Paumanok":

How curious! how real!
Underfoot the divine soil, overhead the sun.

6. See Joseph A. Mazzeo, "St. Augustine's Rhetoric of Silence," *JHI,* 23 (1962): 175–196; reprinted in his *Renaissance and Seventeenth-Century Studies* (New York, 1964), 1–28.

7. Eckhart in Evans, *Meister Eckhart,* p. 247; St. Edmund Rich, *The Mirror of Holy Church* in *The Mediaeval Mystics of England,* ed. Eric Colledge (New York, 1961), p. 139. Colledge explains, p. 136n, that *par corporeles ymaginacyouns,* a mediaeval technical term, very often meant "interpreting metaphors literally." See also Bk. II, ch. XVI of

St. John of the Cross, *Ascent of Mount Carmel,* tr. E. Allison Peers, 3rd ed. (Garden City, 1962).

8. Thomas Carlyle, *Sartor Resartus* (New York, 1937), pp. 219-220.

9. "Although the word, 'symbol,' does not make this immediately clear, the symbol actually participates in the power of that which it symbolizes. The symbol is not a mere convention as is the sign. It grows organically. The symbol opens up a level of meaning which otherwise is closed. It opens up a stratum of reality, of meaning and being which otherwise we could not reach; and in doing so it participates in that which it opens. And it does not only open up a stratum of reality, it also opens up the corresponding stratum of the mind." Paul Tillich, "Theology and Symbolism," in *Religious Symbolism* (New York, 1955), p. 109.

10. For example, Wade, *Thomas Traherne,* p. 175, and Margoliouth, II, 350.

11. Blakney, *Meister Eckhart,* p. 210. Cf. Plato, *Timaeus* 49.

12. In his most valuable and lucid study *Mysticism and Philosophy,* W. T. Stace lists paradoxicality as one of the distinguishing characteristics of both extrovertive and introvertive mysticism. (Philadelphia and New York, 1960), pp. 79, 111.

13. *Six Theosophic Points,* pp. 6-7.

14. Alan W. Watts, *Myth and Ritual in Christianity* (New York, 1960), p. 197.

15. Julian of Norwich, *Revelations,* in Colledge, *The Mediaeval Mystics of England,* pp. 280-281.

16. St. Teresa of Avila, *Interior Castle,* tr. E. Allison Peers (New York, 1961), pp. 28, 194; Dame Julian, *Revelations,* p. 274.

17. For Henry Vaughan's comparable use of this Fountain or Spring symbolism, see R. A. Durr, "Vaughan's Spring on the Hill," *MLN,* 76 (December 1961): 704-707. Even though the Temple and Fountain symbolisms are quite traditional, their pervasive occurrence in the Dobell Folio might seem to be some further evidence of the influence of Herbert and Vaughan on Traherne.

Perhaps, as images of liquids, Traherne's recurrent mentions of Nectar and Wine should also be included in the Fountain group.

18. Cf. Herbert's "Ungratefulnesse": "Where now we shall be better gods then he [the sun]."

19. See Appendix A for a discussion of "Traherne and Renaissance Poetic Theory and Practice."

20. Harold Fisch, *Jerusalem and Albion: The Hebraic Factor in Seventeenth-Century Literature* (New York, 1964), p. 53.

21. *The Paradise Within*, p. 102. See also Martz's discussion of repetition in the *Centuries*, pp. 43–54, and note esp. his view that "the repetitive, digressive, darting movement in both writers [Augustine and Traherne], then, is due to a shared view of the mind's action" (p. 51).

22. Nicolas Cusanus, *Of Learned Ignorance*, tr. Fr. Germain Heron (New Haven, 1954), p. 25. The title inevitably calls to mind Traherne's opening line in "Eden": "A learned and a Happy Ignorance" (p. 12). Cf. Eckhart on learned ignorance in Blakney, *Meister Eckhart*, pp. 107–108.

Chapter Three

1. Cf. John Malcolm Wallace, "Thomas Traherne and the Structure of Meditation," *ELH*, 25 (June 1958): 79–89.

2. *The Confessions*, tr. E. B. Pusey, p. 221. Cf. Eckhart's paraphrase in Blakney, *Meister Eckhart*, p. 132.

3. On stylistic and other grounds, I am inclined to believe that most of the D poems were written later than most of the F poems not found in D.

4. Wade, *Thomas Traherne*, p. 195.

5. OED. For Traherne's extended development of a medical metaphor and for his view that "Mankind is sick" and needs to be spiritually healed see his poem with that opening phrase in *CE*. Cf. Donne's use of "preparatives" in "Satire IV," l. 42. An earlier version of the following reading of "The Preparative" first appeared in *SP*, 61 (1964): 500–521. The University of North Carolina Press kindly granted permission to reprint.

6. Traherne's conception of the infant, "newly clothd with Skin" and dwelling in an Edenic natural world, bears fruitful comparison with Spenser's "naked babes" who in The Garden of Adonis are attired with "fleshly weedes" and move cyclically through the whole pattern of

creation, fall, redemption (*The Faerie Queene*, III, vi, 29–33). See also Wordsworth's *The Prelude*, II, 232–265.

7. Blakney, *Meister Eckhart*, pp. 95–97.

8. *The Cloud of Unknowing*, tr. Clifton Wolters (Baltimore, 1961), chs. 70, 4.

9. Wolters, *The Cloud of Unknowing*, ch. 43.

10. Marie Bonaparte, *Chronos, Eros, Thanatos* (Paris, 1952), p. 12. And Freud: "unconscious mental processes are in themselves timeless"; "in the id there is nothing corresponding to the idea of time." *Beyond the Pleasure Principle*, tr. J. Strachey (London, 1950), p. 33; *New Introductory Lectures on Psychoanalysis*, tr. W. J. H. Sproth (London, 1933), p. 99.

11. Blakney, *Meister Eckhart*, p. 206.

12. *The Sixth Ennead*, IX, 10, tr. W. R. Inge, *The Philosophy of Plotinus*, 3rd ed. (New York, 1929), II, 141.

13. The OED shows that in Traherne's day, as today, perceive is the more general, more inclusive word; conceive means "to take into, or form in, the mind," whereas perceive means "to take in or apprehend with the mind or senses." Gladys Wade cites Philip's *perceiv* as an instance of his "improvements": "The MSS of the Poems of Thomas Traherne," *MLR*, 26 (October 1931): 405, 407. See also Q. Iredale, *Thomas Traherne* (Oxford, 1935), p. 69: " 'The Praeparative' is fairly similar in both versions. Mysterious phrases are made more sensible [by Philip] . . . Presumption is corrected"!

14. *Works of Love*, tr. D. F. and L. M. Swenson (Princeton, 1946), p. 253.

15. *The Republic of Plato* (New York, 1945), p. 223. The nineteenth-century distinction between Platonism as rationalism and Neoplatonism as mysticism was of course not made by the seventeenth-century man (who did not even use the term "Neoplatonism") and is no longer accepted by twentieth-century scholarship. The Platonic distinction between *dianoia* and *noesis*, which was widely developed by Christian commentators, is in several important respects similar to the distinction between psyche and pneuma.

16. Inge, *The Philosophy of Plotinus*, pp. 134, 141.

17. Traherne is using *Intelligence* here and in line 64 in a sense similar to the Neoplatonic Intelligence and to Milton's apposition, "pure Intelligence of Heaven, Angel serene!" (*PL* VII, 181); see Donne's

"The Extasie" and "Goodfriday, 1613. Riding Westward." Traherne's *Simple* means undivided, indivisible, uncompounded, pure, and humble, as well as innocent; OED, s.v. simple. The adjectives of line 20 are a part of what I mean by Traherne's appositive style.

18. Blakney, *Meister Eckhart*, p. 107; and see Evelyn Underhill, *Mysticism*, p. 64.

19. *On Christian Doctrine*, tr. D. W. Robertson, Jr. (New York, 1958), p. 13.

20. Compare Philip's lines 35–36 — which, moreover, seem to contradict his lines 21–23.

21. Evans, *Meister Eckhart*, pp. 412–413. David's saying was a favorite one for Traherne also.

22. Blakney, *Meister Eckhart*, pp. 107, 99.

23. Wolters, *The Cloud of Unknowing*, chs. 5, 25.

24. See, for example, "Innocence," st. 1; *C* I 75; *C* III 7–8; *CE*, pp. 53–54. Cf. William H. Marshall, "Thomas Traherne and the Doctrine of Original Sin," *MLN*, 63 (March 1958): 161–165; K. W. Salter, "Traherne and the Romantic Heresy," *N&Q*, 200 (1955): 153–156; Harold G. Ridlon, "The Function of the 'Infant-Ey' in Traherne's Poetry," *SP*, 61 (October 1964): 630f; and George R. Guffey, "Thomas Traherne on Original Sin," *N&Q*, new series, 14 (March 1967): 98–100. See esp. E. J. Bicknell and J. H. Carpenter, *A Theological Introduction to the Thirty-Nine Articles of the Church of England*, 3rd ed. (London, 1955), pp. 171f on "The Nature of Man," including Article IX, "Of Original or Birth Sin," to which the following paragraph is indebted.

25. *CE*, ch. 32. Although it seems likely, given Traherne' scholarly training and habits, one must grant it is by no means certain from his comments that Traherne carefully read "that arrogant *Leviathan*" (*CE*, p. 261). Like many of his contemporaries, Traherne appears to have reacted strongly to Hobbes and perhaps not altogether without some misunderstanding.

26. Te-shan in *Lien-teng Hui-yao*, 22, cited in Alan Watts, *The Way of Zen* (New York, 1960), p. 131.

27. *The Mystical Theology*, tr. C. E. Rolt (London, 1951), p. 194. Cf. Traherne's use in "The Preparative" and elsewhere of such terms as Disengaged, Empty, Pure, Simple with St. John of the Cross: the soul should "remain detached, empty, pure, simple, as is required for

the state of union." *The Dark Night of the Soul,* tr. K. F. Reinhardt (New York, 1957), p. 62. These terms, as well as Traherne's repeated Naked, Silence, Abyss, and so on, are almost universal among Christian mystics of the negative way.

28. Blakney, *Meister Eckhart,* p. 167.

29. Philip's changing of Thomas' "An Empty and a Quick Intelligence" to the less effective "A quick unprejudic'd Intelligence" loses the key term "Empty" (which Philip had changed in stanza 6, too), and also, as it were, "improves" his brother's morals. Philip's line suggests he may not have taken "Intelligence" in exactly the same sense as Thomas; if so, Philip's stanza also loses the ascending order. See note 17 above.

30. *Biographia Literaria,* ed. J. Shawcross (Oxford, 1907), II, 273.

Chapter Four

1. See Margoliouth, I, xiii–xiv, xxxvii–xxxviii. I favor some time between 1671 and 1674.

2. In accord with the reading of my photostatic copy of the Dobell Folio (Bodleian MS. Eng. poet. C. 42), I have substituted "First" for the incorrect "For" in Margoliouth's text.

3. Pusey, *The Confessions,* p. 131.

4. Richard of Saint Victor, *Selected Writings on Contemplation,* tr. Clare Kirchberger (London, 1957), pp. 138, 136, 139.

5. These and other "sources" are discussed in Arthur O. Lovejoy's valuable essay "Milton and the Paradox of the Fortunate Fall," *ELH,* 4 (1937): 161–179; see also Arnold Williams, *The Common Expositor* (Chapel Hill, 1948), p. 138. It is precisely the double and shifting meanings of Self and Time that make the issue of free will versus determination appear as an unresolvable dilemma or Kantian antinomy. Whereas psyche is bound by and contingent upon clock time and other conventions in the "phenomenal" order of being, pneuma unerringly and spontaneously (that is, with natural, organic freedom) does on the "noumenal" level the will of God which is its own will, as the Father's Will is the Son's, in every eternal Now-moment.

6. For example, I Cor. 1:24, 30; Col. 1:28, 2:3; Proverbs 3:19, 4:7; St. Bonaventura, *The Mind's Road to God,* ch. I, 7–8, tr. George Boas

(Indianapolis, 1953), pp. 9–10; Spenser's "An Hymne of Heavenly Beautie"; Donne's "The Anniversaries"; *Paradise Lost,* III 706, VII 9, 174f. See also Antonio V. Romualdez, "Towards a History of the Renaissance Idea of Wisdom," *Studies in the Renaissance,* 11 (1964): 133–150; and Frank Manley's "Introduction" to *John Donne: The Anniversaries* (Baltimore, 1963).

7. Clark, *Meister Eckhart,* p. 56. See Ch. 3, n. 27 above.

8. It is not necessary to claim that Traherne was familiar with Eckhart's *Commentary,* although it was written in Latin rather than in Eckhart's native German. Whether or not Traherne read it, my point is only that this *Commentary* is very helpful to the critic for understanding "My Spirit."

9. Clark, *Meister Eckhart,* p. 232. And see Augustine's *De Beata Vita,* IV.

10. Clark, *Meister Eikhart,* p. 232.

11. Clark, *Meister Eckhart,* pp. 233–234.

12. And see Clark, *Meister Eckhart,* p. 247: "there is a personal emanation and generation of the Son from the Father." Also *C* II 40–46 and "Church's Year-Book," f. 51v.

13. Boas, *The Mind's Road to God,* p. 38.

14. Clark, *Meister Eckhart,* pp. 243–244. Eckhart's translators have translated *ratio* in Eckhart's text and citations as *idea.*

15. *The City of God,* ed. V. J. Bourke (Garden City, 1962), p. 535. It is noteworthy that in line 45 of "My Spirit" ("And evry Object in my Soul a Thought") Thomas changed "Soul" to "Heart." See Margoliouth, II, 350. Although we cannot determine whether or not Traherne made the change with the biblical or Augustinian passages in mind, this revision appears to be one of several instances in D of changes made by Thomas which Margoliouth should have respected.

16. Many Neoplatonists are both extrovertive and introvertive mystics, though Plotinus is not as clearly and definitely an extrovertive mystic as Eckhart and Traherne are. (See, for example, W. T. Stace, *Mysticism and Philosophy,* p. 77.) With exceptions, Neoplatonists in general tend to reduce or not to share Plato's depreciation (relatively speaking) of the physical sensuous universe, although they can be and have been misinterpreted that way, particularly when the extrovertive purging away of conventional seeing (for the sake of real, regenerated seeing) is mistaken as the introvertive voiding of all

sensuous content. What apparently is missing in or insufficiently stressed by Plato and some Neoplatonists is the extrovertive Hebraic-Christian praise of and joy in God's "very good" visible creation.

17. This controversial stanza could also be validly and valuably, though anachronistically, explained in Berkeleian terms, providing we understand Berkeley not in a Johnsonian sense nor in the usually garbled textbook fashion but rightly in accord with the interpretation of, for example, A. A. Luce, in his *Berkeley's Immaterialism* (London, 1945) and *Sense Without Matter: Or Direct Perception* (London, 1954).

18. Shine is a biblical word especially associated with Christ as well as with the First and Third Persons: see my "Donne's Holy Sonnet XIV," *MLN*, 76 (1961): 484–489, esp. 486, reprinted in my *John Donne's Poetry* (New York, 1966), pp. 251–255.

19. Clark, *Meister Eckhart*, p. 236.

20. Clark, *Meister Eckhart*, p. 237.

21. *Biographia Literaria*, ed. J. Shawcross (Oxford, 1907), I, 202.

22. Clark, *Meister Eckhart*, pp. 236, 58–59.

23. See also, for example, the similar corrupting changes made by Philip in ll. 18–21, 84–85, 117–119. Philip may very well have missed the full implications and allusiveness of Thomas' symbolism.

24. C. E. Rolt, *Dionysius the Areopagite on the Divine Names and the Mystical Theology* (London, 1951), pp. 32–33. To a different end and purpose, Traherne explicitly mentions the inscription in *C* III 56. In the F version of "Ease," uncomprehending Philip changed, as we might expect, "God unknown" to "God most High," necessitating, as Margoliouth notes (II, 355), changes in subsequent lines, which culminate in a meaningless line 28.

Chapter Five

1. Both of these lines are changed to a literal-minded sense in F. Philip apparently did not know that in Platonic mythology, nectar and ambrosia, terms employed repeatedly by Traherne, mean respectively the enjoyment and knowledge of God. See Sears Jayne, *John Colet and Marsilio Ficino* (Oxford, 1963), pp. 89–90, 102, and, on the

metaphor of eating and seeing, Norman O. Brown, *Love's Body* (New York, 1966), p. 167.

2. On imagination and love cf. the concluding Book, XIV, of Wordsworth's *The Prelude,* esp. ll. 168–231. Note that the pattern which *The Prelude* follows (summarized in ll. 194–205) is similar to the basic pattern of the Dobell poems. I quote here ll. 168–170, 188–192, and 206–209:

> By love subsists
> All lasting grandeur, by pervading love:
> That gone, we are as dust . . .
> This spiritual Love acts not nor can exist
> Without Imagination, which, in truth,
> Is but another name for absolute power
> And clearest insight, amplitude of mind,
> And Reason in her most exalted mood . . .
> Imagination having been our theme,
> So also hath that intellectual Love,
> For they are each in each, and cannot stand
> Dividually . . .

See K. W. Salter's fine discussion of "the Highest Reason" (in *Thomas Traherne: Mystic and Poet,* pp. 34–37); he relates it to the Thomistic sense of intellect and (pp. 87–88) to the Cambridge Platonists' conception of Reason. Also relevant is Plato's distinction between *dianoia* and *noesis* and, most relevant, the biblical, mystical distinction between psyche and pneuma.

3. S. Sandbank's excellent article "Thomas Traherne on the Place of Man in the Universe" — pp. 121–136 in *Scripta Hierosolymitana: Studies in English Language and Literature,* vol. XVII, ed. Alice Shalvi and A. A. Mendilow (Jerusalem, 1966) — came to my attention after completion of this chapter. He examines "one aspect of this doctrine [of Circulation] . . . the central position it assigns to man in this dynamic cosmos" (p. 122).

4. See also, for example, "Sixth Day," ll. 61–62, in *Meditations on the Six Days of the Creation,* p. 91, *C* II 90, *C* III 82.

5. Blakney, *Meister Eckhart,* p. 122. Cf. St. Francis de Sales, *Introduction to the Devout Life,* pt. 1, chs. IX, X, tr. John K. Ryan

(Garden City, 1955), pp. 48, 50, and the *Thanksgivings,* pp. 260–263,
6. Robertson, *On Christian Doctrine,* p. 10. See also I Cor. 8:6.
7. See *CE,* chs. XXXII and XXXIII, on gratitude.
8. See James M. Osborn, "A New Traherne Manuscript," *TLS,*
October 8, 1964, p. 928, and Joan Webber, *The Eloquent "I"* (Madison, 1968), p. 223.
9. The phrases are Wade's; see her *Thomas Traherne,* p. 173.
10. Margoliouth, I, xxxii.
11. *The Thanksgivings* frequently use the first four of the couplet's symbols — Image, Friend, Son, Bride — together (pp. 237, 272, 279, 318, for example) as well as separately. See also the Fountain symbolism in Traherne's discussion of love in *C* II 40–42.
The Danaë story of course parallels the Christian story of the conception of a god-man by the extraordinary visitation of a heavenly God and his union with a female human. Also, as the Ganymede allusion (esp. "Drink the Cup") and the images of liquids suggest, "Love" has eucharistic elements in it and is, in its directness and deceptive simplicity though not its tone, somewhat like Herbert's eucharistic "Love III." Notably, the "Stranger" of "The Salutation" has become a "Friend" in "Love."
12. He has, for example, been often criticized for certain repeated rhymes as well as for certain supposedly defective rhymes. Gladys Wade holds, in *Thomas Traherne,* p. 176, that Philip improved the form of his brother's poetry by lessening the frequency of the "Treasure-Pleasure" and "Bower-Power-Tower" rhymes. Having considered Traherne's symbolism, we are in a better position to appreciate even the relatively slight matter of these rhymes: pleasure is (like joy, bliss, felicity) a word which is central and necessary to Traherne's philosophy; treasure, bower, and tower are a part of his major symbolism, and therefore are inevitably and appropriately recurrent. Moreover, upon examination, Wade's criticism turns out to be without any real foundation, another of the many gratuitously derogatory criticisms of Traherne: in the 22 poems which occur in both D and F, the only poems on which Wade can base her judgment, Philip reduces the "Treasure-Pleasure" rhyme (which appears 13 times: 4 in the singular, 9 in the plural) only *once,* and does so by simply omitting Thomas' lines ("Silence," lines 61–62) probably because of their sense and not because he wishes to lessen the frequency of the rhyme. The "Bower-

Power" rhyme occurs only 3 times (how can Wade think this frequent?) and only once does Philip get wholly rid of it, this time by substituting a clumsy, conventionally pious, and unpoetic pair of lines for Thomas' poetic lines ("The Estate," lines 27–28). Once Philip changes "Power-Bower" to "Power-Tower" ("My Spirit," lines 101–102). "Tower-Power" appears only once; Philip makes no change. The comparisons I have made lead me to believe that often when Philip has been credited with improving the poetry by correcting rhyme, meter, and so on, he is primarily concerned to change the meaning and only very rarely effects an actual poetic improvement — and in some of these rare instances he may have simply followed Thomas' corrections in the lost manscript. It should also be noted that, given Traherne's themes, the expletives in his poetry often function as one necessary device for achieving emphasis and intensity and for helping to create the aura of childhood. See the critically helpful notes by Edward Nicholson, "Treherne [sic]: Curious Rimes to 'Joy,' " *N&Q,* 3 (March 25, 1911): 232, and Margoliouth I, xxxviii–xxix.

13. John Rothwell Slater, ed., *Of Magnanimity and Charity* (New York, 1942), p. vii. Allan H. Gilbert, "Thomas Traherne as Artist," *MLQ,* 8 (1947): 446–447. See also Margoliouth I, xli.

14. *The Essential Plotinus,* tr. Elmer O'Brien, S.J. (New York, 1964), p. 170. I have used O'Brien's translation of this passage because it seems to me much clearer than Mackenna's. Christian commentators on Plotinus associated his second hypostasis, the Intelligence, with the Second Person of the Trinity.

15. Robertson, p. 12.

16. T. S. Eliot, "The Metaphysical Poets," *Selected Essays,* 3rd ed. (London, 1951), pp. 286, 287. Consider Traherne's "I did feel strange Thoughts" in "Dumnesse," p. 42.

17. Margaret Willy, *Three Metaphysical Poets* (London, 1961), p. 36. Another reading of sts. 2 and 3, alternative to the one I shall present, might regard them as expressive of the dark night of the soul.

18. Cf. Northrop Frye on Blake in *Fearful Symmetry* (Boston, 1962), p. 431: "The real apocalypse comes, not with the vision of a city or kingdom, which would still be external, but with the identification of the city and kingdom with one's own body."

19. *Mysticism,* p. 437.

20. With this discussion of joy, love, and union or communion in

Traherne, compare K. W. Salter, *Thomas Traherne*, ch. IV, esp. p. 61, and Itrat Husain, *The Mystical Element*, pp. 297f for different views. It is noteworthy that Dorothy L. Sayers, distinguished scholar and translator of Dante, includes Traherne along with Dante and Blake among those who attained to the Beatific Vision, the Vision of God which is the end of the mystical way; see her "The Beatrician Vision in Dante and Other Poets," *Nottingham Mediaeval Studies*, II (1958), 6, 22. See also *Meditations on the Six Days of the Creation*, pp. 51–52 (and "The Sacrifice of a Devout Christian," pp. 393f in Part III of *A Collection of Meditations and Devotions* — "The Sacrifice" is perhaps the one part of Part III which has the best claim to being Traherne's); also see the *Thanksgivings*, pp. 229, 235, 241, 260, 277, 289, 312–313, 315–316; and *C* II 1, 17, 18, III 40, 60, 95–100. In explaining, at the end of *C III*, "what it is to be the Sons of God and what it is to live in Communion with him," Traherne is describing, I believe, the unitive stage. (See esp. *C* III 99, and cf. Underhill, *Mysticism*, pt. 2, ch. X, "The Unitive Life.") Traherne could offer this description to Susanna Hopton or to whomever he addressed the *Centuries* because, I think, he had lived in and enjoyed union; like the anonymous author of *The Cloud of Unknowing*, Traherne was a master of achieved vision instructing a novice who wished to travel the *via mystica*.

21. With this concluding prayer in "Thoughts IV," ll. 95–102, and with l. 5 of "Goodnesse," "The Face of God is Goodnesse unto all," compare the phrasing in the concluding prayer of "Meditations on the Fourth Day's Creation," in *A Collection of Meditations and Devotions*, p. 54. With the first stanza of "Goodnesse" compare the *Thanksgivings*, pp. 221–222.

22. Similarly, Herbert's lyric sequence "The Church" ends with "Love III," a communion poem, which in its last three lines contains the paradox of serving and being served. Compare also Herbert's "The Agonie," st. 1, "The Bunch of Grapes," and "Love-joy." On universal sacrifice see esp. the concluding paragraph of chapter XI, "Of Goodness," in *CE*, p. 86. The paradox of gain through loss appears most explicitly in "Goodnesse," st. 3.

23. *Revelations*, pp. 281, 277.

24. In Vaughan's "Joy of My Life," for example, we read, "Stars

are of mighty use . . . Gods Saints are shining lights." Traherne very clearly uses "Stars" as a symbol of redeemed men in, for instance, *Meditations on the Six Days of the Creation*, p. 50. In sts. 2, 5, and 6 of "Goodnesse," Traherne appears to use "Stars" sometimes literally, sometimes symbolically, and sometimes both at once. Cf. Traherne's use of "Lillies" in "Goodnesse" with his use in *Meditations on the Six Days of the Creation*, pp. 45, 77; *The Thanksgivings*, p. 286; and "The Person," l. 45.

25. Blakney, *Meister Eckhart*, p. 130.

26. See also, esp., ch. XI, "Of Goodness," in *CE* and p. 251. There are many pertinent sections in *C*, esp. I 71–76, IV 26–29, 55. Cf. G. M. Hopkins' "As kingfishers catch fire."

Appendix A

1. To this end, I am especially indebted to Joseph A. Mazzeo, "A Seventeenth Century Theory of Metaphysical Poetry," *Romanic Review*, 42 (1951): 245–255; "Metaphysical Poetry and the Poetic of Correspondence," *JHI*, 14 (1953): 221–234; "A Critique of Some Modern Theories of Metaphysical Poetry," *Modern Philology*, 50 (1952): 88–96. The first two essays are reprinted with some changes in Mazzeo's *Renaissance and Seventeenth-Century Studies* (New York, 1964), pp. 29–59. I am also indebted to S. L. Bethell, "The Nature of Metaphysical Wit," *Northern Miscellany of Literary Criticism*, 1 (1953): 19–40, reprinted in *Discussions of John Donne*, ed. Frank Kermode (Boston, 1962), pp. 136–149. See also ch. III of Benedetto Croce's *History of Aesthetic* in *Aesthetic*, tr. Douglas Ainslie (New York, 1958), pp. 189–203.

2. Tesauro, quoted by Bethell, *Discussions*, p. 141. In one form or another, Traherne could have acquired the idea that the world is a poem of God from Plotinus or the Stoics as well as from Tesauro. See Mazzeo, *Renaissance and Seventeenth-Century Studies*, p. 53, and, as noted by Mazzeo, Rosamund Tuve, *Elizabethan and Metaphysical Imagery* (Chicago, 1946), p. 159.

3. Bethell, p. 149. As with later English Neoclassicists, wit is primarily concerned with order, both in and outside the poem; for example, Pope's "An Essay on Criticism," ll. 232–252. This raises in-

teresting questions about the differences, real and supposed, between the Metaphysical and Neoclassical poem.

4. Mazzeo, *Romanic Review,* p. 249.

5. Douglas L. Peterson, *The English Lyric from Wyatt to Donne: A History of the Plain and Eloquent Styles* (Princeton, 1967); and A. K. Foxwell cited by Kenneth Muir, ed., *Collected Poems of Sir Thomas Wyatt* (Cambridge, Mass., 1963), p. xxii. Wyatt's psalms were printed by John Harrington and Thomas Raynauld in 1549, but not included in Tottel's *Miscellany,* 1557.

6. The phrase "pure simplicity" is from Sonnet 28 in *Astrophel and Stella.* See also Sonnets 1, 3, 6, 15, and 74. See Louis Martz's important study of Sidney's probable influence on Herbert, *The Poetry of Meditation,* pp. 259–282. For Herbert's use of apposition in his "Prayer," see E. B. Greenwood, "George Herbert's Sonnet 'Prayer': A Stylistic Study," *Essays in Criticism,* 15 (1965): 27–45; note esp. Greenwood's "Appendix on Apposition as a Mode of Expression," pp. 43–44.

Appendix B

1. Baltimore, 1963, p. 20.

2. Joseph Campbell, *The Hero with a Thousand Faces* (New York, 1956), p. 39.

3. Alan W. Watts, *The Supreme Identity: An Essay on Oriental Metaphysic and the Christian Religion* (New York, 1957), p. 132.

4. *Ibid.,* p. 143.

5. Richard Maurice Bucke, *Cosmic Consciousness* (New York, 1961), p. 14.

6. Norman O. Brown, *Life Against Death* (New York, 1959), pp. 86, 84. Recently, Professor Malcolm Day kindly directed my attention to his unpublished doctoral dissertation, "Thomas Traherne and the Perennial Philosophy," Western Reserve, 1964 (not listed in *Dissertation Abstracts*). It contains valuable insights and is the kind of study which will enhance understanding of the perennial or universal character of Traherne's work.

Index

Aelred of Rievaulx, St., 47
Ambrose, St., 109
Apposition or appositive style, 93, 130–133, 155–156, 170, 193; and catalogs, 53, 55, 58, 67, 71, 75–76, 120, 157–158, 173–174, 186
Aquinas, St. Thomas, 26, 29, 58
Aristotle, 14, 29, 33, 122, 126, 211n20
Athanasius, St., 19
Augustine of Hippo, St., 6, 105, 152, 166; in Traherne's tradition, 13, 14; region of unlikeness, 19; nearness of God, 25, 62, 166; negative theology, 26, 42; on evil, 29–30; redeemed vision, 82, 128; original sin, 86–87; cited by Eckhart, 122, 126, 129

Bacon, Francis, 54
Beachcroft, T. O., 10
Beatific vision, 80, 152, 174–175, 224n20
Bell, H. I., 3–4, 5, 11
Berkeley, George, 89–90, 166, 220n17
Bernard, St., 10, 27
Bible, 13, 14, 16–17, 35, 105; and Traherne's symbolism, 47–53; its other influence on Traherne, 55–56; Traherne's study of, 110–111, 208n4. See also John 1; Genesis 1
Blake, William, 22, 35, 38, 55, 69, 102, 194, 224n20
Boehme, Jacob, 13, 14, 27, 47
Bonaventura, St., 6, 13, 26, 57, 126, 130

Bradley, F. H., 166
Bremond, Henri, 20–21
Bridgman, Sir Orlando, 158
Brown, Norman O., 200–201
Browne, William, 195
Bruno, Giordano, 191–193
Bucke, R. M., 199–200, 201

Campion, Thomas, 142
Carlyle, Thomas, 43
Catalogs, 38–41, 53–56, 82, 107; and symbols, 43, 53, 58, 64, 71, 75–76, 120, 141–142, 174; and appositions, 53, 55, 58, 67, 71, 75–76, 120, 157–158, 173–174, 186
Catherine of Genoa, St., 21
Chaucer, Geoffrey, 194
Childhood theme, 15–18, 23–24, 28, 29, 31, 38, 44, 61f; criticism of, 8, 9; and Perennial Philosophy, 198–201
Circulation, doctrine of, 148–153
Cloud of Unknowing, The, 13, 71, 84, 223n20
Coleridge, S. T., 93, 130
Communion, see Union
Concentrated image: defined, 43. See also Symbols, pneuma-revealing
Contemplation, 6, 10, 42, 71, 84, 161, 163, 181, 184; distinguished from meditation, 107–108. See also Meditation
Coomaraswamy, Ananda, 197
Cornford, F. M., 79